God, Israel, and Shiloh

We Strongly Endorse...

Dr. Pat Robertson
Chairman & CEO of The Christian Broadcasting Network
Host of The 700 Club

David Rubin lives in the biblical heartland of Israel and stands on the frontlines of the battle against Islamic terrorism.

His book gives a unique insight into the heart of those brave modern pioneers settling the land of the Bible as foretold by the ancient Hebrew prophets.

Rabbi Dr. Shlomo Riskin
Chief Rabbi, Efrat
Chancellor, Ohr Torah Stone Colleges and Graduate Programs

God, Israel, and Shiloh by David Rubin is a magnificent testimony of the faith and courage expressed by our contemporary generation of pioneer heroes. Every one of its pages is soaked in the blood and tears of daily sacrifice, but is imbued with the odyssey of love and faith which brought the Rubin family back to God and back to Israel, while it placed them at the forefront of contemporary Jewish history.

I believe it is a must read for anyone who wants to understand the uniqueness of our very unique and fateful generation of return.

Rabbi Dr. Sholom Gold
Rabbi Emeritus Kehilat Zichron Yoseph, Har Nof, Jerusalem
Dean, Avrom Silver Jerusalem College for Adults

God, Israel, and Shiloh is an extraordinary chronicle of the Divinely-ordained return of Jews to their roots and to their ancestral Land. It presents, in very readable fashion, the human and historical background, and the sincere religious commitment and perseverance of the heroic inhabitants of Judea and Samaria, despite the terrorism and other obstacles in their path.

From the ancient hills of Shiloh comes a passionate voice expressing a remarkable clarity of vision about the challenges facing Israel. David Rubin's powerful words should be heard and listened to.

MK Binyamin Elon
Former Member of the Knesset and Minister of Tourism

In this extremely important work, David Rubin takes us on a fascinating spiritual journey through Jewish history, from the exodus from Egypt all the way up to both the tragic and miraculous events in recent years in Israel.

The return to the ancestral lands, the acute pain of terrorism, and the misguided peace plans are clearly explained by one who not only reads about, but experiences first hand, these amazing events every day.

God, Israel and Shiloh is essential reading for anyone who wants to know the facts on the ground from the heartland of Israel.

Dr. Mordechai Nisan
Lecturer of Middle East Studies
Hebrew University of Jerusalem

David Rubin has written a gripping biblical and historical narrative about the Land of Israel, as a stirring saga of the Jewish people and the quest for redemption. *God, Israel, and Shiloh* resonates with moving personal stories, psychological insights, and compelling political commentary. This book is about faith and struggle, Judaism and Zionism – woven around the special sacred site of Shiloh, then and now. David Rubin is writing, living, and making Jewish history in Israel. An exceptional masterpiece and a must read.

God, Israel, and Shiloh

Returning To The Land

by

David Rubin

God, Israel, and Shiloh
ISBN: 978-09829067-2-9

Published by Shiloh Israel Press

Copyright © 2011 by David Rubin
First edition published 2007. Second edition 2008.

Contact The Author
david@ShilohIsraelChildren.org
1-845-738-1522

Contact The Publisher
sipress@ShilohIsraelChildren.org

For Orders:
1-800-431-1579 (toll-free)

Websites:
www.ShilohIsraelChildren.org
www.DavidRubinIsrael.com

Book Production: Chaim Mazo
Cover Design: Infinity Concepts and Leah Ben Avraham

Printed in Israel

Dedication

This book is dedicated to the memory of all of the children of Shiloh, and all the others, who did not survive the terror attacks, whose lives were brutally taken from them for the "crime" of living as Jewish children in the heart of the Land of Israel.

Noam Apter

Avi Sutton

Har-El Bin Nun

Gila Sara Kessler

Shmuel Yerushalmi

Yehuda Shoham

Yonatan Eldar

Avihu Kenan

About The Author

David Rubin is a former Mayor of Shiloh, Israel, and a long time resident who lives with his wife and children on a hilltop overlooking the site of ancient Shiloh. He is Founder and President of Shiloh Israel Children's Fund, established after he and his three-year-old son were wounded in a vicious terror attack. He is a powerful spokesman for the "settlers" in the Biblical heartland of Israel, as well as for the victims of terrorism. David has spoken to many Jewish and Christian audiences across the United States, Europe, and in Israel. He has appeared on Fox News, Newsmax and other TV networks, as well as on radio and in print media.

Contents

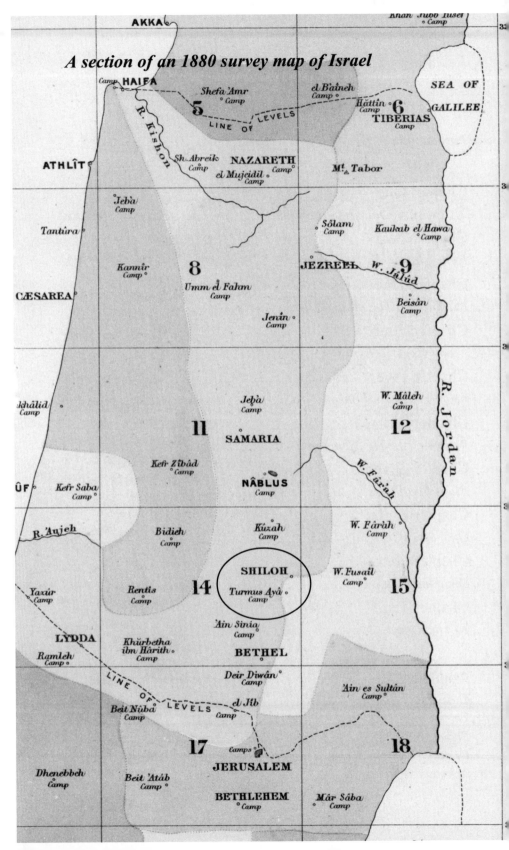

A section of an 1880 survey map of Israel

Introduction

Blood was gushing out of my leg like an open fire hydrant in an inner-city neighborhood. The car had gone totally dead and we were rolling down the road. I turned the ignition and it didn't start, and they were still shooting!

A scene from a horror movie perhaps? No, this was a real-life experience that I could never have foreseen or even dreamed about just twenty years earlier, while I was still living in the United States.

Many people living in America have their own moments of frightening experiences, but one who moves to Israel soon comes to realize that life in Israel is like no other place in the world. From the constant threat of war and terrorism to the often unstable economy in which salaries never seem to rise; from the constant security checks to the prayer services in crowded bus stations, life is clearly experienced on another plane. Then again, the Nation of Israel is like no other nation.

What other nation has been enslaved, then after a miraculous escape, been given the Bible, which has become the all-time bestseller; established its nation in a Land that God sent it to, been driven from its Land and scattered around the world for almost 2,000 years, eventually returning to that tiny territory to re-establish a sovereign nation once again, all exactly as forecast by the Prophets of the Bible? Is this a normal nation?

"But you Israel are my servant, Jacob whom I have chosen, the seed of Abraham, My beloved." (Isaiah 41:8)

It's clearly no exaggeration to say that Israel is in the news far more than most nations, and way out of proportion to its size. Is this just by some chance of nature? Some would insist that it's a natural consequence of Israel's so-called abuse of the rights of the Palestinians. Others would say that it's somehow a result of anti-Semitism, and therefore, Israeli actions are, quite unfairly, always under a microscope. There are certainly other theories on this question, which we will discuss in this book, but there is no disputing the disproportionate attention that Israel receives in the world media.

The terms "West Bank", "Palestine", and "Settlements" have all become practically household terms in homes across the United States and in many other countries, but I would venture to say that most people have no clue where the terms actually come from, what they represent, and the history behind them. Semantics often seems a fascinating linguistic game played by editors and journalists, but in the Middle East, it is also a dangerous game which frequently touches on life and death issues.

In Israel especially, the power of words cannot be underestimated. As a transplanted American Jew who wasn't born or raised in Israel, but decided to live there on my own, and personally experienced the pain of terrorism along with my three-year-old son, all of these questions have deep meaning to me. In fact, there is virtually no issue in Israel that doesn't stir heated debate.

Perhaps, it's a consequence of being a nation whose very existence, or at least right to exist, is questioned every day, but the intensity of daily discussions about current events can often be quite fierce. Many tourists riding the local buses in Israeli cities for the first time, are surprised every top of the hour to hear the volume of the news reports turned way up for all riders to hear, as if all passengers need to immediately know the latest event. But it's all a reflection of the ever-present feeling in Israel of the precarious but meaningful nature of life.

In Israel, hardly a day goes by without peace plans discussed in the news. At the same time, hardly a day goes by without at least an attempted terror attack.

Let's create a hypothetical situation in which a creature from a distant planet comes down to Earth and settles down in Israel. I am convinced that he would be totally perplexed by this strange country. From the daily news reports, one hears about the frantic diplomatic activity and peace summits, while simultaneously, rockets are falling on Israeli cities, teenagers are being shot at while standing at bus stops, and there is internal confusion as to how to respond. Is this a normal people? And does it make any sense?

My intention in this book is to shed new light on the role of the Jewish people in history, traveling through time with this often stubborn, but resilient and creative people.

We will explore from Biblical times to the present, and will focus on the implications of past and present events in Israel for the future of Israel and the world. As you may have expected, I will tell this story from a perspective which is not often heard in the mainstream press, but which has great significance for the current conflicts in Israel and the free world.

From my hilltop home on a street overlooking the ruins of the ancient city of Shiloh, I often gaze into the scenic valley of Shiloh, and when I do, I see its ancient history coming to life in the present-day life of its people. In the midst of its tranquility, I relive its many Biblical stories and the rich history of this Land that I call home, for without the Biblical and historical context, we are simply walking in circles, with no real sense of direction.

There is more to life than simply "living for the moment," as any Israeli in touch with his roots will tell you. When viewed in the proper context, the abnormality of the Jewish People makes perfect sense, as does the media obsession with Israel.

Let's explore the amazing history of this peculiar nation called Israel, sharing in its glory and tragedy of the past, its painful conflicts in the present, and its vision of hope for the future. Its relationships, both with the world and with its God are relationships that have relevance and implications for all of us. Let's read...

David Rubin

God, Israel, and Shiloh

"The entire assembly of the Children of Israel gathered at Shiloh and erected the Tent of Meeting there, and the Land had been conquered before them, but there was left among the Children of Israel seven tribes that had not yet received their inheritance."

Joshua said to the Children of Israel, "How long will you wait, to come and possess the Land that the Lord, God of your fathers has given you?"

(Joshua 18:1-3)

Chapter One

My Personal Journey To Shiloh

"Bring us back to you, Lord, and we shall return, renew our days as of old."

(Lamentations 5:21)

In July of 2005, while on a speaking tour in the United States, I stayed for several days in a community called Shiloh Greens, rode in a car on a street called Shiloh Road, and while listening to a radio, I heard several advertisements for Shiloh Inns (which I ended up staying in on a subsequent trip). As a resident of the community of Shiloh in Israel, all this was fascinating to me.

As one who also grew up in the United States, I am quite familiar with American history, and this was a clear reminder of the Biblical foundations of the United States. The nation whose currency clearly states "In God We Trust", derived that belief from the Bible of Israel, and there is no place more central to the Bible than the Land of Israel. As a result of this, there is an abundance of places in the United States with names that are derived from the Bible. There are cities called Bethlehem, Hebron, and Jerusalem.

There are at least 65 cities, towns, or villages in the United States called Shiloh. In addition, there are many places of worship, prayer books, parks, schools, a child of movie stars Angelina Jolie and Brad Pitt, two movies, a Civil War battle, and an old Neil Diamond song, all with the Shiloh name. Most of the name-givers probably don't know the origin of the word, but the roots of America are Biblical and the abundance of Shilohs is not purely coincidental.

To me this raises many questions about the current and ongoing dispute between Israel and its enemies over the Biblical heartland of Israel.

♦ What is, or should be, the role of those Americans who believe in the significance of the bestselling book of all time, the Bible?

♦ Who are the settlers?
♦ Who are the Palestinians?
♦ What are the occupied territories, and who is occupying them?
♦ What is the real Shiloh, the original Shiloh all about?
♦ Finally, why are the words "Israel" and "the West Bank" household terms, and why are they seen and heard almost daily in the American media?

There are political ramifications for all of these questions, as well. During the tenure of former Israeli Prime Minister Ariel Sharon, he referred to the deep historical significance of Shiloh on numerous occasions, paradoxically suggesting that Israel might have to part with important, historic, and strategic places like Shiloh and Beth El, because of the overwhelming international pressure on Israel for concessions that supposedly can't be resisted. A short time later, after a great uproar in Israel and after Knesset Speaker Reuven (Ruby) Rivlin made a very public and supportive visit to Shiloh, the Prime Minister suddenly backtracked, vowing that there will always be Jews living in Shiloh and Beth El, referring to these places as "the cradle of the Jewish People."

Clearly, this is not just a simple dispute about some pieces of real estate. The battle for Shiloh is a microcosm of the battle for the entire Land of Israel, while the battle for the Land of Israel is a microcosm of the free world's battle against Islamic terrorism. Yes, it is a dispute that has ramifications for the entire world, and Shiloh is at its center.

Shiloh is a town which possesses amazing natural beauty and spiritual significance. It is the cradle of Jewish civilization and nationhood, the source of Jewish prayer and worship, and the epitome of Israel's faith. Shiloh has always been a magnet for believers from around the world. It is the city that is referred to in the Talmud as "the resting place," and the place that is considered by most Biblical commentators to be synonymous with the coming of the Messiah.

In modern political parlance, many people would call Shiloh "an obstacle to peace," as it falls in the heart of a region that some people have designated as a future "Palestinian state." Others would call it "the front lines in the war against terrorism" for the same reason. It is a place that one cannot be neutral or apathetic about, and for that reason the media flocks to Shiloh often, and there is a steady flow of enthusiastic Jewish and Christian tourists despite the danger of Arab snipers on the roads.

However one describes the significance of that place in the heart of the Samarian hills, in the Biblical portion of the tribe of Ephraim, it doesn't even begin to explain the more personal side of Shiloh; specifically, how this relatively assimilated Jew (among many others) from the United States of America came to live in the "West Bank settlement" of Shiloh, on a street that overlooks the site of Ancient Shiloh, marrying and raising his family there, participating in its public life, suffering for the privilege of living on its hills, and building for its future.

Our journey begins in a middle class neighborhood in Brooklyn, New York, which is where I was born and raised. This was a predominantly Jewish, but non-religious neighborhood, the kind of place where the only Jewish hero that most people knew about was baseball Hall of Famer Sandy Koufax, where eating in non-kosher Chinese restaurants was an almost weekly ritual, and where synagogue attendance was a once-a-year obligation on Rosh HaShanah and Yom Kippur. I went to public schools in Brooklyn and other parts of New York and, in short, grew up as a more or less average American boy in New York, playing a lot of basketball and other sports, watching a lot of sports on television, and eventually, going to a lot of 1970s rock, folk-rock, and jazz concerts, and dabbling in the drug culture associated with it. I lived through the era of deteriorating neighborhoods and rising crime rates in the streets of New York, and my family moved a couple of times as a result of that. I remember my entire neighborhood in Brooklyn being severely shaken by "the apple pie murder" in the luncheonette across the street from my house, when the owner, who happened to be a Holocaust survivor, was asked by an early morning customer for a piece of apple pie. When he said that he didn't have any, he was shot dead on the spot.

Through all of these somewhat ordinary or not so ordinary happenings in the childhood and adolescence of this American child, there were certain things that set me apart from the American mainstream. For one, there were the holidays. Christmas season was always a time of great confusion for me. After all, here I was, an average American kid, and every year I was confronted with the dilemma of how to relate to this fascinating, colorful holiday that took over the stores every year for several weeks, dominated the television every year for several days, took over the decor of the streets for several weeks, and caused us to have a weeklong vacation from school. However, it was always made clear to me that whether or not I wanted to participate in the excitement, it wasn't mine. This was not an insignificant yearly reminder for me, because I was a public school student. I was part of the vision of the great American "common school," which was designed to create the great American melting pot. This term meant, in effect, that those who could, would blend into the mainstream of American society, and differences would be minimized in favor of the common good. The problem was (and still is for so many American Jews) always how to fit in and feel a part of this major American holiday without actually participating. If at all possible, it was certainly no easy task. Little did I know at that time, and quite ironically, that the millions of Christian Americans who were celebrating this holiday, were in reality rejoicing over the birth of a Jewish carpenter, one who lived 2,000 years ago in Bethlehem, in the Land of Israel!

Another part of my life that set me apart was what was ironically called "Hebrew School." This particularly American Jewish phenomenon was actually a supplementary after-school school. Despite its name, it didn't teach its students to speak nor to understand the holy tongue. Nor was Bible learned in any meaningful way. The People of the Book, who brought the Torah (Bible) down from Mt. Sinai, thus enlightening the entire world, created a sad caricature, by teaching their children to read a few parts of the Holy Book and the basic prayer book, but only by rote, with little or no comprehension, for the sole purpose of preparing for the great, expensive Bar (or Bat) Mitzvah bash that would occur a few short years later. The Bar/Bat Mitzvah is a religious ceremony welcoming the 12 or 13-year-old child into adulthood. Now we all know that a child of that age is not an adult, not even physically. The adulthood status refers to the child's taking on of the responsibility for following God's commandments. Sadly, for the Hebrew School child, the emphasis is on the big party that follows, because the ceremony usually marks the end of any formal Jewish education. This anomaly, a person of the Book who is ignorant of the Book, is one of the great tragedies of American Jewish life. The People that was given the lofty task to be "...a kingdom of ministers and a holy nation" (Exodus 19:6), created hundreds of thousands of Jews who couldn't answer the simple question, "Why is it important to be a Jew?"

The inevitable result was an intermarriage rate hovering around the 50% mark and surpassing it in many parts of the country, causing the Jewish population in the U.S. to gradually, but steadily decrease over time. Most Jews could give no compelling reason not to marry out of the faith, and in the case of intermarried Jews, despite occasional exceptions to the rule, they didn't succeed in passing along their heritage to the next generation. That isn't to say that the non-Jewish spouses were not wonderful people, but the role of Israel (the Jewish people) was to be "a light unto the nations" (Isaiah 49:6), a spiritual and moral example for the rest of the world. This is an extremely difficult task to fulfill in general, but as a tiny minority assimilated (intermarried) into a Gentile society, it is nearly impossible.

"...And you shall be holy unto Me for I the Lord am holy and have set you apart from the peoples that you should be Mine." (Leviticus 20)

Anyhow, I nearly became one more statistic in the intermarriage trend. Even though most of my friends were Jews, I didn't hesitate to date others. If Judaism wasn't a big part of my life, why should it matter to me? I had a non-Jewish girlfriend for some time when I was in my mid-twenties and I really saw no reason not to pursue it further. I figured that if the woman I eventually married really loved me, she would learn from whatever cultural Jewish traits I had and I would learn from her background, as well.

During my mid-twenties, several pivotal events occurred in my life, although at the time I was certainly not aware of their significance. In 1980, when I was 23 years old, I traveled through Europe by myself by train, meeting other young people along the way. I decided to detour south to Morocco, as what I assumed would be an interesting divergence to a third world country. It didn't occur to me that an Arab, predominantly Moslem country could possibly be inhospitable to a Jew. As the train moved into Morocco, things started to get interesting. I was traveling in a train car that consisted of several six-person compartments. The young people in my compartment were from Germany, and we got along quite well. Not that it was a concern of mine, but they stressed to me that they were different than their parents and/or grandparents who were somehow connected to the Nazi death machine that had slaughtered six million Jews in World War II.

The Germans were only some of the people that I met on that train. In the adjacent compartment was a group of Moroccan youth, returning to Morocco from Belgium, where they were university students. Dressed in jeans and drinking beer, they appeared to be quite friendly and we hit it off. Once during our conversation, a police officer came into the compartment and one of the students quickly handed me his beer. Afterwards, he explained to me that as Muslims, alcoholic beverages were illegal for them, but not for tourists. At another point during our conversation, I asked them if they would like to meet my German friends. One of the young Moroccans, who had introduced himself to me as Rashid, responded sharply, "We don't like them." I, of course, pointed out to him that he hadn't even met them, so how could he make such a statement? He answered, "Because of Munich. The Germans killed our people!" He explained that he was referring to the 1972 Munich Olympics, when 11 Israeli athletes were held captive and eventually murdered by Palestinian Arab terrorists. The German police subsequently killed five of the terrorists. I sensed that Rashid's blanket antipathy towards Germans stemmed from the death of the terrorists who were killed, which puzzled me, since these young Moroccans seemed so modern and westernized, so how could they identify with terrorists? I responded, "But Rashid, you're Moroccans. How can you feel bad for the terrorists?" He looked me in the eye with a frightening, violent stare that I will never forget, raised his fist in the air and shouted, "Because Jerusalem is for all the Arabs!!!" I felt a chill from head to toe as he said these words, perhaps because I suddenly felt vulnerable as a Jew with this group of Arabs, whose "friendship" I had naively thought transcended what I then considered to be unusually closed-minded thinking for the twentieth century.

In June of 1982, I was called for jury duty in Brooklyn Criminal Court. This basically involved sitting in a huge room for a week, waiting to be called, or not to be called, for a court case. That week also happened to be the breakout of Operation Peace for Galilee, or the war in Lebanon. This was the war which was Israel's response to the Palestine Liberation Organization's (PLO) missiles that had been falling on the Galilee and to the terror attacks that had been launched from terrorist bases in Lebanon for years. In one particularly horrifying attack on an elementary school in Maalot (in northern Israel) several years prior, 21 schoolchildren had been murdered and 78 people wounded.

I found myself glued to the newspapers, which were filled with dozens of articles about every detail of the fighting in Lebanon, and since I wasn't getting called into any court rooms, I had lots of time for reading. I had always been a news buff and I loved to read current events, but this time it was different.

As I sat in the Brooklyn Criminal Court building reading each stage of the battles, I felt as if I was flying on every Israeli attack plane and dodging every enemy missile. I felt an emotional attachment to Israel that was not just some news junkie's passion for the excitement of a good story. Later that week, I had a long conversation with my non-Jewish girlfriend, and she asked me what I thought about what the Israelis were doing in Lebanon. I responded that they were trying to prevent missiles from PLO terrorists in Lebanon from falling on the northern Israeli communities, as well as terrorist infiltrations of these communities. I remarked that Israel had to finally respond after years of PLO terror on Israeli civilians. I also said that Israel should drive (then PLO chairman) Yasser Arafat and his terrorists out of Lebanon. To this she responded, "Well, you know that (then Israeli Prime Minister) Menachem Begin is also a terrorist!" We then had a big argument about her comparison. When I finally hung up the phone, I was shaking, not because of any special affinity for, or loyalty to Menachem Begin, but due to my awareness of the intensity of my emotions, and the possible implications of all of this, with ramifications that I certainly couldn't foresee at that time. The process of spiritual awakening that had apparently started in Morocco began to pick up steam after that phone conversation.

As I said earlier, up to that point, I had considered myself a fairly close to average American young adult, following the sports teams, avidly listening to rock, folk-rock, and jazz music, and experimenting here and there with the various recreational drugs of the generation. I was living in the "here and now," in the modern world, and the last thing I expected was to be drawn into what I perceived to be the primitive world of Judaism, a world that had always appeared to me to be somewhat archaic and not relevant to my life, or to modern society at all. For several years, I had considered myself an atheist, claiming that all religion was akin to a dogma of superstition that was created by man to make him comfortable with his existential dilemma. Later on, at a friend's suggestion, I had explored, not in any great depth, some of what is referred to as eastern philosophy, which kind of helped to change my status from atheist to agnostic. Now in 1982, partially as a result of a war on the other side of the world, I was suddenly confronted with a culture and a history and a state, called Israel, concepts that seemed somehow both foreign and new to me, but that I was drawn to like a magnet that I couldn't resist.

I began to seek any information that I could find about Israel. My parents, and especially my father, who was a proud Jew and had always dreamed of visiting the Jewish homeland, were happy to further my discovery process. Sensing the changes that were going on in my head, they gently encouraged me to join them for a visit to the Jewish Museum in New York, where I was suddenly confronted with people and places in Jewish history that I had never been exposed to, such as King David, King Solomon, and the Holy Temples that once stood in Jerusalem.

"Then Solomon gathered together the elders of Israel and all the heads of the tribes, the leaders of the ancestral families of the Children of Israel, to King Solomon in Jerusalem, to bring up the Ark of the Covenant of God from the City of David, which is Zion." (1 Kings 8:1)

For the first time in my life, I began to understand, or at least to feel, that I was a part of a people with both a glorious and tragic history, and perhaps present and future, although I certainly wouldn't have been able to explain it at that moment. Over the next two years, I began a process of exploration and voracious reading, devouring any book I could get my hands on about Israel, Zionism, and Jewish history. I even began to tentatively read some basic books about Jewish religion and philosophy. Simultaneously, I took a few courses in Jewish history, learning about the Jews of Eastern Europe. This was where my grandparents had immigrated to the United States from, so I threw myself into a period of intensive and extensive research of my family history. I traveled from cemeteries to libraries, from where I could get genealogical information, to the homes of great aunts and uncles and grandparents, to the long-abandoned Jewish neighborhoods in Brooklyn and Manhattan, trying to find out everything that I could about my family history, which, I had somehow thought, didn't go back further than two generations. Years of persecution, dislocation, and immigration had apparently taken their toll on American Jews, most of whom knew that their not so distant roots went back to Eastern Europe (in most cases), but usually didn't know much more than that. For instance, until I started my research, I knew virtually nothing about my family history before the Holocaust, and certainly knew little about Jewish history before the years of Nazi persecution and mass murder. I learned a lot from all of my research and reading, but a few key lessons stand out. Firstly, in my family research, I read about the now mostly extinct Jewish communities of Eastern Europe, who despite widespread poverty, large families, and persecution from the Gentiles around them, did not engage in street crime and, for the most part, were upstanding, loyal citizens in the countries in which they dwelled. How poor were they? My great uncle and great aunt differed in their relative assessments of the community's poverty, but the common yardstick they separately chose was chicken:

> "Most people struggled to make a living. On Friday nights, we could sometimes have a little chicken to eat, but in the middle of the week we couldn't afford to have chicken and things like that. This was a luxury. When somebody went in the middle of the week to take a chicken to the *shochet* (ritual slaughterer), he would ask, 'Is someone not well in your house?' because if someone wasn't well, you had to feed them chicken soup!"
>
> *Edward Modlin, 1983*

> "In Druya (their town in Russia), we used to have chicken for Passover and Sukkot. When I came to America, and my sister gave me a quarter of chicken, I looked at her and said, 'Rosie, chicken in the middle of the year? And a whole quarter. That's enough for four people!' There were some richer people in Druya who maybe ate better, but most people were very poor there."
>
> *Rebecca Modlin Cohen, 1984*

The lack of street crime and the general family and social cohesion in their communities was an eye-opener for me, because where I grew up in New York, poverty, large families, and street crime seemed to go hand in hand. What was the cause of their general optimism, intact family life, and social morality despite their often difficult living conditions, which in most American cities would cause many to despair or lash out at others? The answer soon became clear to me: Their religious lifestyle, based on their commitment to the laws of the Torah, was the source of their faith, optimism, and relative social cohesion.

Simultaneous to all of my research which was slowly pulling me closer to a more traditional lifestyle, I had started teaching in a Brooklyn inner-city public school, where there were few white teachers and virtually no white students. Going into it, I had no qualms about the ethnic mix, or lack thereof, but when I started to take off from work for Jewish holidays, the black principal turned on me, and apparently working together with her sidekick, a Black Muslim social worker, did everything in her power to make me feel uncomfortable and force me out of the school. It was a blatant case of what a black colleague of mine, an outstanding veteran teacher, referred to as "reverse racism," but I felt powerless to fight it, and was advised by the union leaders to use the opportunity to switch to a better school and a more friendly atmosphere. It turned out to be sound advice, but the truth is that a lot of good had come out of that difficult experience. The principal used to focus much of the school's educational program on what she referred to as "Black Pride." The entire school used to chant every morning together with the principal, "I am black, and I am proud!" Needless to say, the one white boy in my class had a confused expression on his face every time he had to chant these words, but by this constant focus on ethnic pride, I was encouraged to look inward and examine my own identity. This process was further reinforced on the one or two occasions when the principal made what I considered to be blatantly anti-Semitic remarks in front of all the children and teachers. So here was a situation which at the time was very upsetting for me, but paradoxically acted as an impetus for my process of introspection and exploration into my heritage.

"Who is wise? He who learns from every person." (Ethics of the Fathers 4:1)

Another lesson learned in my period of initial exploration was the connection between Judaism and Zionism. Zionism was the political movement, begun in the late 19th century, to encourage the return of the People of Israel to the Land of Israel where they would create a modern Jewish state in the Land of Israel, or, as the world then called it, Palestine. It was eventually established in 1948 mostly by secular, socialist Jews who, influenced by the Russian Revolution and Marxism, set out to create a secular Jewish state, what the first Prime Minister, David Ben-Gurion, proudly called "a nation like all the other nations." However, unbeknownst to its secular founders, God had other plans, and revealed His divine presence in many ways in the early years of the state and up to this very day. By learning about these miracles, both revealed and hidden, which impacted the rise of the State of Israel and are still ever-present in our lives (see later chapters), and the prophecies that were fulfilled or are being fulfilled in our times, I became convinced that the connection between Zionism and Judaism was integral and inseparable. Ultimately, one cannot survive without the other, no matter how hard American Jews or secular Israelis may try. God has called His children home, and is trying to guide us to follow His anointed role for us.

"...For from Zion will come forth Torah and the word of the Lord from Jerusalem." (Isaiah 2:3)

"See, I (Moses) have taught you decrees and ordinances, as the Lord my God has commanded me, to do so in the midst of the Land to which you come, to possess it." (Deuteronomy 4:5)

I realized that in order to be true to my newfound beliefs, I needed to adopt a Torah-true lifestyle and to live in the Land of Israel. I felt that one without the other would be incomplete and a lack of intellectual honesty on my part. However, this was no easy task. Following the commandments required an almost total transformation of my lifestyle to adapt to the kosher dietary laws, the complex rules of Shabbat (the Jewish Sabbath), and sexual discipline (abstinence) before marriage. Up to that point, I would have eaten what I desired whenever I desired it, including my favorite foods – shrimp, lobster, and cheeseburgers – all forbidden foods according to Jewish Law. Now I would have to restrain my culinary desires and forego some of my favorite foods. The change was not easy, and I often found myself yearning for my previous diet.

The rules of Shabbat were totally foreign to me, and it required a long learning process until I began to grasp the simple, yet profound concept that by placing strict restrictions on our behavior for that 25 hour time period (no television, no computer, etc.), we actually create for ourselves the freedom to focus on the things that really matter. Similar in principle was the once foreign concept of sexual abstinence before marriage, or even before the third date! The thought that intense sexual passion too soon can actually prevent a relationship from developing in a healthy, natural way had never occurred to me. By taking the focus off sex, we put the emphasis on the personal chemistry without which no relationship can grow. As any happily married couple can tell you, a healthy sex life is based on love and caring, not on advanced sexual technique.

Those were the personal, internal challenges. Next came the practical challenges of the move to Israel. On my first visit to Israel, I met some of my Israeli cousins for the first time. They were very friendly and welcoming, but I remember being disturbed by a few of their comments to me. In our very first get-together, after I told them of my plans to take courses in Judaism, I was immediately told, "In Israel, you don't have to be religious." I was later informed by my other cousin that, "One of the worst things that someone in Israel can do is to become religious." Fortunately, I ignored their advice, and I spent two consecutive summers learning in Israeli yeshivas (religious seminaries) and took a year and a half leave of absence from my New York City teaching jobs to continue that learning. This was an exciting time for me, filling in the basics of Jewish knowledge and Hebrew that I couldn't learn on my own. After those eighteen months, I returned to the U.S, planning to quickly return to Israel. Even so, it took me several difficult years to finally leave the country that still felt like home in so many ways.

Once I had finally made the permanent move to the Land of Israel, known as Aliyah (literally "going up", in Hebrew), there were the difficulties of living in what was still for me, a foreign culture to some extent. Learning Hebrew with its different alphabet, opposite direction, and unusual (for an American) pronunciations was quite an adjustment for one who had never experienced the benefit of receiving a full Jewish education growing up. Then there were the economic challenges and uncertainties in an often unstable economy in which wages hardly ever go up, but daily expenses frequently do. The social reality was different, as well, especially back then. As opposed to most westernized countries, like the United States and the European nations, there appeared to be a palpable lack of manners in the streets. One could often witness people pushing and shoving while waiting to get on a bus or enter a government office. Such behavior, which was quite normal in the Middle East, was at first disturbing for this American immigrant. However, I soon noticed that if someone would faint and fall down, people would be falling over each other to help the person to get up and to give him medical advice. These were only a few of the new and often overwhelming peculiarities or norms of Israeli life that I had to adjust to. It took me several challenging years in Israel until I could finally say that I was settled into my new lifestyle and culture.

Arriving in Israel as a thirty-five year old single, I started out by returning to my yeshiva (religious seminary) in Jerusalem and living in its dormitory. But I knew that this was but a temporary solution and frankly I was long over-ready to move on to the next phase in life. Within a few months, I saw an old brochure whose words jumped out to me, "Before there was Jerusalem, there was Shiloh." I opened up a Tanach (Bible) and was captivated by the almost magical history of Shiloh, where God's presence in the Land was evident for 369 years. Shiloh was the center, where the Tabernacle had stood for those 369 years, where the great leader Joshua preached to the tribal elders, where Hannah the Prophet had prayed for a child and where that son Samuel the Prophet grew up and served the Almighty, eventually but powerfully delivering God's word, both to the kings of Israel and to the ordinary people.

Shiloh was also a modern community, where the first Israeli pioneers had taken up the challenge of settling and developing the Biblical heartland just fourteen years earlier. In 1992, after a Sabbath visit in October and after just four months in Israel, I moved into a caravan (no-frills stationary trailer home) in Shiloh, the first capital of Ancient Israel. I was finally home, living right in the heart of the Land that God had promised to Abraham our forefather and Moses our teacher and prophet, thousands of years before. Within a few months, with the voluntary help of a talented matchmaker, I met the woman who would soon become my wife, and we were married a few months after that. Within a few short years, I became involved in the public life of the community, bringing a touch of American initiative and idealism to an already pioneering community. I served the community as its mayor (in a voluntary, but elected capacity) and was also active in improving its educational system. A few short years later, I personally experienced the horror of terrorism, eventually turning that trauma into a positive venture for the children of Israel. However, my greatest pleasure has always been simply to walk up and down the ancient boulders of Shiloh and to explore its hills and its past, both with my children and with visitors from abroad. This is best done with Bible in hand, for the hills resonate with our glorious and often tragic history. In short, that is my personal story. But again, you may ask, how did this tiny, peculiar people called Israel come to be mentioned in the news almost every day? Why are the "crimes" of Israel debated in the United Nations almost every day? And why do events in the Middle East often leave the most brilliant minds perplexed and lacking workable solutions? Despite their bitter years of slavery in Egypt, all of their wanderings, the persecution over the centuries, the Holocaust, and all of the modern wars, how and why did this unusual people survive?

"If the statistics are right, the Jews constitute but one percent of the human race. It suggests a nebulous dim puff of star dust lost in the blaze of the Milky Way. Properly the Jew ought hardly to be heard of; but he is heard of, has always been heard of. He is as prominent on this planet as any other people...The Egyptian, the Babylonian, and the Persian rose, filled the planet with sound and splendor, then faded to dream-stuff and passed away; the Greek and the Roman followed, and made a vast noise, and they are gone; other peoples have sprung up and held their torch high for a time, but it burned out, and they sit in twilight now, or have vanished...All things are mortal but the Jew; all other forces pass, but he remains. What is the secret of his immortality?"

(Mark Twain, from his article, "Concerning the Jews")

To even attempt to answer these questions, it is essential to know some of the remarkable history: of this unusual people called Israel, of the Land of Israel, and of the Bible of Israel. Let's read on...

Chapter Two

From Slavery To The Land

"I am the Lord, your God, Who has taken you out of the land of Egypt, from the house of slavery."

(Exodus 20:2)

One of the most common expressions in Jewish prayer is "in remembrance of the Exodus from Egypt." We frequently thank God "...who took us out of the land of Egypt." Even though we as individuals weren't there, we perform the Passover Seder every year to commemorate that event.

"You shall not eat leavened bread with it (the Passover offering), for seven days you shall eat matzah (unleavened bread) with it, bread of affliction, for you departed from the land of Egypt in haste – so that you will remember the day of your departure from the land of Egypt all the days of your life." (Deuteronomy 16:3)

The Jewish holidays are based on the Hebrew calendar, so every year the date is different (or seems to be), but Passover (Pesach in Hebrew) usually falls in April. The Seder is an evening-long festive meal lasting several hours, and includes the recitation of the story of the Exodus from Egypt, songs of praise, concrete culinary rituals, and lots of role-playing.

It is incumbent upon each of us on the Passover holiday to remind ourselves that we as a nation were miraculously taken out of Egypt and out of the bondage of slavery. We recall the Ten Plagues that the Almighty inflicted on the Egyptians as a not-so-subtle incentive to persuade Pharaoh to let us leave Egypt. We eat the matzah, the unleavened bread, for the entire holiday, to remind us of the haste in which our ancestors were forced to leave the land of their bondage. We recall as well, the miraculous splitting of the Red Sea, which enabled the escape from Egypt. As you can see, Passover is a major event in the Hebrew calendar, in which we, in effect, renew our national-religious covenant with God.

"Why do we eat bitter vegetables? Because the Egyptians made our ancestors' lives bitter." (The Passover Haggadah)

"In every generation, each person must feel as if he personally had gone out of Egypt, as the Torah says, 'You should tell your child on that day, saying, 'When I left Egypt, the Lord did great miracles for me.' Not just our ancestors were redeemed by God, but also us, as the Torah says, 'And He took us out from there, in order to bring us to the Land of Israel and to give us the Land that he promised to our forefathers.'" (The Passover Haggadah)

This recognition of the great suffering that we as a people endured followed by the incredible miracles that God performed for us at the Red Sea and throughout the Exodus, and the bond of covenant that was created through all of this; this is a constant theme in Jewish prayer. In fact, the entire seven-day holiday of Passover, is totally dedicated to the covenantal bond between Nation and God that was created by the Exodus.

It's interesting to note that the month of Nissan (see Glossary), in which Passover falls, is often referred to as the first month in the Hebrew year, even though the first month is actually Tishrei, the month of Rosh HaShanah (the Jewish New Year). This is because the Exodus from Egypt represents the birth of the Jewish nation as a unique nation with a special bond to the Master of the Universe. At my family Seder each year, we all put on those cute little cone-shaped shiny birthday hats, with the elastic string under the chin. The children always enjoy anything that has to do with costumes, but the lesson is more important than the novelty. We are actually celebrating the birthday of the People of Israel as a nation, so in the spirit of Passover, we celebrate in a concrete, easily understandable way. All of our adult guests can and do enjoy the fun, but the focus is on the children and the educational experience.

After leaving Egypt and experiencing the miraculous splitting of the Red Sea, among other miracles, the Children of Israel came to Mt. Sinai, where their leader and Prophet Moses received the Ten Commandments. He also received the knowledge and inspiration from God that would be needed to write down almost all of the first five books of the Torah (Bible). Jews affirm this divine act over and over when they raise the Torah in the air in synagogue after the thrice weekly public Torah reading, proclaiming in unison, "This is the Torah that Moses placed before the Children of Israel, from God's mouth to Moses' hand."

In addition to the Written Law (the Pentateuch, the Prophets, and the Writings), which often needed clarification, Moses was given a series of explanations and detailed instructions, based on principles that were to be passed down from generation to generation. This came to be known as The Oral Law, because even its basic principles weren't written down until the eventual second Exile was imminent in the year 70 of the Common Era, when it was feared that the traditions would be lost. The resultant massive written text that was eventually compiled, over a period of several hundred years, became known as the Talmud, or learning.

Hence, on Mount Sinai, the Children of Israel, who had officially become a nation at the Exodus from Egypt, were now given their raison d'etre, their reason for existence, and their Holy Book to guide them. The nation of Israel was not meant to be a "nation like all the other nations," but a nation with a specific purpose, a position of spiritual responsibility and leadership. It was an awesome responsibility, one that was not to be taken lightly as some storybook fantasy.

"And now, if you hearken well to Me and observe My covenant, you shall be to Me the most beloved treasure of all peoples, for Mine is the entire world. You shall be to Me a kingdom of ministers and a holy nation. These are the words that you (Moses) shall speak to the Children of Israel." (Exodus 19:5-6)

It was not just Moses who witnessed this most historic of events on Mount Sinai. The entire nation stood at the foot of the mountain and knew that this was no ordinary climb up a hill. They were witnessing what no other nation had ever seen before. The People of Israel are God's witnesses in this world, on whose shoulders rest the task of revealing His presence and greatness.

"The entire people saw the thunder and the flames, the sound of the shofar and the smoking mountain; the people saw and trembled and stood from afar." (Exodus 20:15)

The noted philosopher and rabbinical scholar Eliezer Berkovits wrote an impressive analysis of the previously unheard of concept of a special religio-nation, set apart from all the others. This idea is and always has been unique to Israel, but has often been misunderstood, causing great confusion about the role of Israel in this world.

"As a rule, religions do not make nations. Nations and peoples are biological, racial, and political units. They will accept a religion, but the religion they accept is accidental to the national group. Christianity, for instance, created no people; peoples already existing as such, accepted Christianity. The same applies to other world religions. Israel alone is a people made to fulfill a God-given task in history; the people whom, as Isaiah expressed it (Isaiah 43:21), God 'formed' for himself."

(Eliezer Berkovits, Faith After The Holocaust, P.147)

Israel is indeed a religio-nation that was formed through sacred covenants, first with each of the Patriarchs Abraham, Isaac, and Jacob, and finally at that majestic moment when the entire nation of Israel witnessed the fire on the mountain, in effect witnessing the giving of the Law to Moses on Mt. Sinai. This was essentially a national confirmation of what had been promised previously to the ancestors of what would soon become a holy nation.

The King of the Universe chose Israel as His unique people and promised them the Land of Israel, simultaneously demanding their obedience to the words of His Torah. This was the Eternal Covenant, **which was not always universally adhered to, but was never abrogated, neither by God nor Israel.**

Despite this, the ongoing marriage between Israel and its Maker, to borrow an analogy from the wise King Solomon, has had its ups and downs. The Children of Israel, often referred to in the Bible as a stiff-necked people, didn't wait long before their first rebellion. Time was passing as Moses stood on the mountain in the presence of the Holy One, and the Children of Israel, waiting impatiently for their leader's descent from the mountain, and beginning to think that he was dead, began their first great rebellion against the Lord, building a huge statue of a Golden Calf, that they intended to worship. The mob mentality which led to the mass participation in this act of rebellion was encouraged by the riff-raff, the many rabble-rousing pagans in their midst, who had taken a free ride out of Egypt with God's Chosen People. On the other hand, to their great credit, the women of Israel, intuitively understanding the lack of basic faith and loyalty represented by this rebellion, refused to participate and protested against their husbands' foolishness (see Midrash Tanchuma: Pinchas). The building of the Golden Calf was an appalling act of idolatry, thereby defying the clear prohibition against idol worship. The men of Israel, who had just witnessed the most amazing of miracles before and during the Exodus from Egypt, failed a test of faith in a moment of weakness. At that very moment, God informed Moses of what was occurring at the foot of the mountain. Moses, fearing that the harshest of punishments would be the result of such a sin, was terrified for the survival of his People, and pleaded with the Lord, begging and even demanding of the Almighty to have mercy on them.

"Why Lord, should Your anger flare against Your people, whom You have taken out of the land of Egypt, with great power and a strong hand? Why should Egypt say the following: 'With evil intent did He take them out, to kill them in the mountains and to annihilate them from the face of the earth?' Relent from Your flaring anger and reconsider regarding the evil against Your people." (Exodus 32:11-12)

When Moses finally descended the mountain, he himself was shocked to actually see His People, spurred on by the agitators of little faith, worshipping the Golden Calf. Yes, it had been upsetting to hear about it, but to see it with his own eyes was terribly shocking for this man who had just a moment ago experienced God's presence. He smashed (or dropped, depending on which Biblical commentary one reads) the stone tablets of the Ten Commandments on the ground, perhaps from anger, or perhaps accidentally because he was so upset.

Upon reaching the bottom of the mountain, Moses set the Golden Calf on fire, burning it to the ground. He ascended the mountain once again, and again asked the Almighty to forgive the people's idolatry. Moses' plea was heard, but God insisted that those idolaters of Israel would be punished for their sin. Nonetheless, the Holy One reiterated the Covenant with the entire Children of Israel, including their eventual possession of the Land of Canaan (Israel). He agreed that His presence would remain with the Children of Israel forever and that He would perform great miracles for them as they continued their sojourn in the desert for forty years, and of course, as they eventually entered the Land of Israel. However, this divine protection would not be unconditional. The Almighty demanded of Israel many responsibilities (mitzvot) that could only be expected of a nation that had a covenant with its God, outlining the basic principles to be followed upon entry into the Land. In addition, He warned Moses of many of the pitfalls that they would encounter along the way.

"He said, 'Behold! I seal a covenant: Before your entire people I shall make distinctions such as never have been created in the entire world and among all the nations; and the entire people among whom you are will see the work of the Lord, which is awesome, that I am about to do with you. Beware of what I command you today: Behold I drive out before you the Amorite, the Canaanite, the Hittite, the Perizzite, the Hivvite, and the Jebusite. Be vigilant, lest you seal a covenant with the inhabitant of the Land to which you come, lest it be a snare among you.'" (Exodus 34:10-12)

These prophetic words and clear warnings for the future, as well as the potential lessons to be learned by the future generations were told "face to face" to Moses. The great leader of Israel, his face now literally glowing with the radiance of God's presence, descended Mount Sinai once again. It is said that the light was so brilliant that it was impossible for people to look directly at his face. He descended this time with the new stone Tablets of the Ten Commandments in his hands. This was the seal of the covenant between the Lord and His People.

The Ten Commandments included the most central guidelines of civilization: the commandment to worship the one God, to keep the Sabbath day holy, to honor one's parents, to be faithful towards one's spouse, not to steal nor to murder, to refrain from jealousy toward one's neighbor, and more. These are only some of the most basic principles given to Israel via Moses on Mount Sinai that in our times have been informally adopted and internalized by Western civilization as its own.

The Children of Israel then built the portable Tabernacle, the moveable site of worship that was to accompany them throughout the next forty years in the desert and onward. They built it according to the precise specifications that God had given to Moses.

"They shall make an Ark of acacia wood, two and a half cubits its length; a cubit and a half its width; and a cubit and a half its height. You shall build it with pure gold, from within and from without shall you cover it, and you shall make on it a gold crown all around." (Exodus 25:10-11)

"You shall make a Menorah of pure gold...Six branches shall emerge from its sides, three branches of the Menorah from its one side and three branches of the Menorah from its second side... " (Exodus 25:31-32)

"See and make, according to their form that you are shown on the mountain." (Exodus 25:40)

It was built with their own Hebrew labor and repentance, and with their gifts (gold, silver, and copper contributed by the people). The entire project was under the guidance of their God, via His prophet and servant Moses. Within the Tabernacle would rest the Holy Ark of the Covenant, and within the Ark would sit the stone tablets with the Ten Commandments carved into them. The Israelites would take the Tabernacle from place to place with them throughout their wanderings in the desert. Its portable materials made it easily transportable. The cloud that hovered over the Tabernacle made it clear that the Lord's presence would remain with them at all times, as long as they proved themselves worthy.

"The cloud covered the Tent of Meeting, and the glory of God filled the Tabernacle. Moses could not enter the Tent of Meeting, for the cloud rested upon it, and the glory of God filled the Tabernacle. When the cloud was raised up from upon the Tabernacle, the Children of Israel would embark on all of their journeys. If the cloud did not rise up, they would not embark, until the day it rose up. For the cloud of God would be on the Tabernacle by day, and fire would be on it by night, before the eyes of all of the House of Israel throughout their journeys." (Exodus 40:34-38)

The portable Tabernacle was, for the Israelites in the desert, almost like a caring, sensitive parent, needing to walk his young child to nursery school and back, then to a friend's house to play, then perhaps on to the next activity. With a young child, every "journey" requires encouragement to support the little one's developing ego and sense of autonomy. So it was for the nation of Israel in its "infancy and early childhood stage." Every step needed guidance from above, and assurance that the Almighty was with them, just as youngsters need constant reassurance from their parents, as they try to develop as autonomous individuals in an often frightening adult world.

The Israelites were to perform various kinds of sacrifices in the Tabernacle as a sign of their devotion to the Creator, but also as a sign of repentance for their sins. The Lord gave Moses specific instructions as to how and when this was to be carried out. The sacrifices, or offerings, were ongoing, but the holidays were a time for special and additional offerings to God. The Children of Israel's sojourn in the desert lasted a total of forty years. During that time, the Lord used Moses as His conduit, to teach His People the laws of the Torah. This included the personal commandments such as the dietary laws (kashrut), and the social commandments, such as the need to be especially kind to strangers, widows and orphans.

"You shall not taunt nor oppress a stranger, for you were strangers in the Land of Egypt. You shall not cause pain to any widow or orphan. If you at all afflict them, and they cry out to Me, I will surely hear their cry..." (Exodus 22:20-22)

Then of course, there were the national commandments, such as the imperative to eventually conquer and possess the Land of Israel, and all of the national commandments pertaining to various aspects of life and livelihood in the Land of Israel. Taking on new responsibilities and challenges was not easy for this spiritually intense, but stiff-necked (stubborn) people. They frequently despaired of the self-sacrifice demanded of them and their faith was tested time and time again. They often complained of the difficulties of life as a wandering nation in the desert.

"There was no water for the assembly, and they gathered against Moses and Aaron. The people quarreled with Moses and spoke up, saying, 'If only we had perished as our brethren perished before God! Why have you brought the congregation of God to this wilderness to die there, we and our animals? And why did you bring us up from Egypt, to bring us to this evil place? Not a place of seed, or fig, or pomegranate; and

there is no water to drink!'" *(Numbers 20:2-5)*

Moses, feeling the pain of His People as any good leader should, went with his brother Aaron, who was also the high priest in the Tabernacle, and they fell on their faces at the entrance of the Tent of the Meeting. The glory of the King of kings appeared unto them. Moses was instructed to speak to a rock in front of the people, and water would come forth from the rock, providing nourishment for the Children of Israel and their animals. More importantly, their faith in the Lord's miracles and faithfulness would be restored.

Sadly, Moses was the one who failed to live up to this test of faith that the Almighty had given him. Rather than speak to the rock, he struck the rock twice with his staff. Yes, water gushed forth in abundance, providing physical sustenance for the people, but Moses, the great leader, having failed to sanctify God's name in the eyes of His People by doing exactly what he had been instructed to do, lost the privilege of leading His People into the Land that was to be their eternal inheritance. That lofty privilege, and great responsibility, was to fall on Yehoshua Bin Nun (Joshua, son of Nun), his anointed successor.

You might ask why Moses, whose spiritual level wasn't attained by anyone else in Jewish history, was punished for such a minor distinction. I once heard this compared to the relative mistakes in war of a brigadier general and a corporal in the military. When it comes to following orders in the midst of battle against the enemy, the brigadier general should ideally be held to a much higher standard. What is for the corporal a serious but forgivable error becomes for the brigadier general a major sin. Furthermore, the important lesson imparted through Moses was so crucial for the Children of Israel; that God's commandments are to be adhered to without rationalization, exactly as they are intended to be. The centrality of this lesson for Israel, and indeed for all of humanity, even outweighed the personal wishes and hopes of Moses, the great leader of Israel.

"Moses went and spoke these words to all of Israel. He said to them, 'I am a hundred and twenty years old today; I can no longer go out and come in, for God has said to me, 'You shall not cross this Jordan (River).' The Lord, your God – He will cross before you; He will destroy these nations from before you, and you shall possess them. Joshua – he

will cross over before you, as the Lord has spoken " (Deuteronomy 31:1-3)

At that point, Moses had just finished writing down the words of the Torah for His People, for the Torah was to guide them into the Land of milk and honey that the Lord their God had promised to them. They were to follow its precepts and ordinances in the Land to which Joshua would lead them. After the death of Moses, God made the bold declaration to Joshua that would give him the spiritual fortitude to meet the monumental challenge that stood before him at that moment:

"Moses My servant has died. Now arise, cross this Jordan, you and this entire people, to the land that I give to them, to the Children of Israel. Every place upon which the sole of your foot will tread I have given to you, as I spoke to Moses. From the desert and this Lebanon until the great river, the Euphrates River, all the land of the Hittites until the Great Sea toward the setting of the sun will be your boundary." (Joshua 1:2-4)

"Only be very strong and very courageous, to observe to do, according to the entire Torah that Moses My servant commanded you; do not deviate from it to the right or to the left, in order that you may succeed wherever you will go. This Book of the Torah shall not depart from your mouth; rather you should contemplate it day and night in order that you observe to do according to all that is written in it; for then you will make your way successful, and then you will act wisely." (Joshua 1:7-8)

That was the recipe for success that the Almighty gave to Joshua as he prepared to enter the Land of Israel. The minimal boundaries of the possession in the Land that it clearly laid out for them included all the land from the Mediterranean Sea to the other side of the Jordan River all the way into present-day Jordan and Iraq, and parts of Syria. Furthermore, it implied the possibility of additional conquests (Every place upon which the sole of your foot will tread...)

However, it wasn't an unconditional gift. It was a two-fold promise whose degree and pace of fulfillment would depend on the people's willingness to adhere to both of its components. The first, belief in the Lord's promise, faith that His words were true, was essential to the success of their mission, but the mission couldn't be carried out in a quick and painless fashion without the spiritual road map of the Torah guiding them as to how to proceed along the way. The level of difficulty encountered in the Land would be directly contingent on their adherence to God's commandments, both the personal ones that regulated each individual's daily life, and the national commandments that would govern our dealings with the nations that controlled the Land at that time. That was (and remains to this day), the dual challenge for Israel, to conquer, possess, and dwell in the Land of Israel, but to follow God's commandments within it. Only thus, can Israel fulfill its mission.

"Beware for yourselves, lest your heart be seduced and you turn astray and serve gods of others and prostrate yourselves to them. Then the wrath of the Lord will blaze against you; He will restrain the heaven so there will be no rain, and the ground will not yield its produce; and you will be swiftly banished from the goodly Land that the Lord gives you." (Deuteronomy 11:16-17)

As we will read in the coming chapters, this was not only a warning; but a prophetic vision as well, for it reflected the ongoing spiritual struggle that was to determine the ups and downs of Israel's existence in the years to come.

The lessons delivered to Israel through Moses in the Sinai Desert were a spiritual road map for the Israelites of that time period, but not only for that time period. Its basic principles and precepts were the Torah of Life, guidelines that were intended to be adhered to by all of the future generations of Israel.

The sheltered existence of the Children of Israel in the desert was an abnormal state, a temporary period of early childhood growth for God's children, during which all of their needs were taken care of by the Creator. But it couldn't last forever. As with any child, they had to grow up and move on to the next wonderful stage of growth, which would be exciting and uplifting, but filled with great peril and challenges to be met as they entered the Land of their inheritance.

"He (Moses) commanded Joshua son of Nun, and said, "Be strong and courageous, for you shall bring the Children of Israel to the Land that I have sworn to them, and I shall be with you." (Deuteronomy 31:23)

Chapter Three
Dwelling In The Land

"The entire assembly of the Children of Israel gathered at Shiloh and erected the Tent of Meeting there..."

(Joshua 18:1)

The famous God-directed conquest of the Land was carried out by the great leader Joshua Bin Nun. The falling of the walls of Jericho and the Battle of Ai were among the highlights of the conquest which had occurred while Gilgal was the capital, but the time had come to move on once again. After the fourteen years that the people and their portable Tabernacle had been based in Gilgal, Joshua decided that it was time to have a more permanent existence in the Land, and he led His People to Shiloh, located on the great north-south mountain ridge in the portion of the tribe of Ephraim, about 20 miles north of what is now Jerusalem. This was no accident, as the regions of higher elevation were always considered to be more secure from enemy attack. Furthermore, Shiloh was adjacent to, and just to the east of, the pivotal, strategic, and historic Road of the Patriarchs. The portable Tabernacle of the desert had been brought to Shiloh, but the decision had been made that this would be the long-term resting place, that the periodic wanderings of the desert would be brought to an end. Thus, the Tabernacle to be established in Shiloh would be built of stone walls, as opposed to the collapsible wooden walls from the wanderings in the desert. The Children of Israel had come home, and the "Wandering Jew" would no longer be homeless.

Joshua Bin Nun

"...And the Land had been conquered before them, but there was left among the Children of Israel seven tribes that had not yet received their inheritance. Joshua said to the Children of Israel, 'How long will

you wait to come and take possession of the Land that the Lord, God of your fathers has given you?'" (Joshua 18:1-3)

Several questions can be raised about this powerful exhortation, really a reprimand, from Joshua to the Children of Israel:

♦ Why did Joshua choose the hills of Shiloh to reprimand his People about the crucial mitzvah (commandment) of taking possession of the Land?

♦ Why did he do it at this particular time?

♦ What is the relevance of this reprimand for our times?

♦ What is the role of Shiloh in our times regarding the imperative to take possession of the Land?

While the latter two questions will be dealt with in later chapters, it's helpful to examine a map to see the geographic implications of

The Road of the Patriarchs:
Viewed from Shiloh

the location of Shiloh in the Land of Israel. Shiloh, as we've already mentioned, is positioned along the strategic north-south road called the Road of the Patriarchs (today's slightly rerouted and repaved Road 60). This is the road that the Patriarchs most likely rode their donkeys on in Biblical times. It was always the main north-south road, winding its way through the curves of the hills and valleys of the rocky terrain. As we said, the road has been rerouted slightly in our times to make it straighter and to avoid some of the more dangerous Arab areas, where a Jew who wants to live dare not enter, but to this day it

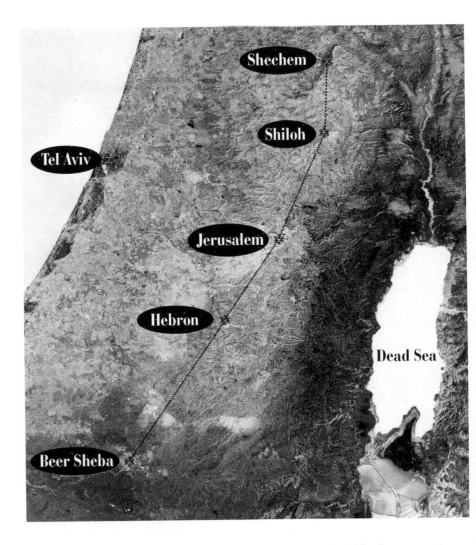

The Road of the Patriarchs from Above: *The axis of Israel's Biblical cities starting on the Mountain Ridge of the heartland and moving southward on the Road once traveled by the Biblical leaders in Israel.*

is essentially the same north-south road that extends from Beer Sheba through Hebron to Jerusalem, then on to Shiloh. From Shiloh, the road continues on to Shechem and from there northwards. Furthermore, Shiloh is accessible from the coast and from the north (the Galilee). It is also located near a body of flowing water, the Shiloh Creek, which extends from Shiloh all the way to the coastal region. Joshua certainly thought of all these factors, but of course the fact that Shiloh is in the portion of Ephraim didn't hurt, since Joshua was from Ephraim. For all of these reasons, as well as its central geographic location, it was the ideal place from which to urge the Children of Israel to go out in all directions and actively claim their inheritance in the Land.

When the Children of Israel arrived in Shiloh, they were coming to a city that was already built up. According to the excavations carried out by archeologist Israel Finkelstein (See Biblical Archaeology Review: January/February 1986), Shiloh was already an established Canaanite city during the period of the Patriarchs Abraham, Isaac, and Jacob.

Extensive remnants of tools and pottery have been found which are dated from that period. In addition, there exists to this day, the remains of a massive wall from the Canaanite period in Shiloh, which indicate that Shiloh was a walled, hence protected, city at that time. It should be pointed out, however, that when Joshua and His People came to Shiloh, "the land was conquered before them" (Joshua 18), which seems to indicate that there was either very limited Canaanite settlement in Shiloh by the time the Israelites arrived, and/or there was no resistance when Joshua and his forces arrived to take control.

According to Finkelstein, the Canaanites probably left because of famine. Therefore, when Joshua brought His People to Shiloh, he was choosing a city that was already fairly well fortified, conveniently and centrally located, and easy to take control of. As we've already mentioned, Shiloh was also in the heart of the inheritance of the important tribe of Ephraim, which Joshua belonged to. All of these factors together made Shiloh an ideal place, at least in Joshua's eyes, to create the first capital for the Chosen People in their new Land.

As for the timing, we need to look at the context. The Land was, to a great extent, under Israel's control, but there were many pockets of resistance throughout the Land. In fact, the land was still very much in dispute. There remained many hostile forces well-entrenched in the Land and it was urgent that the people not become complacent, lest they lose what had already been achieved. The warning had already been given before the entry into the Land:

"The Lord spoke to Moses in the plains of Moab, by the Jordan, at Jericho, saying: Speak to the Children of Israel and say to them: When you cross the Jordan to the land of Canaan, you shall drive out all of the

inhabitants of the land before you; and you shall destroy all their prostration stones; all their molten images shall you destroy; and all their high places shall you demolish. You shall possess the Land and you shall settle in it, for to you have I given the Land to possess it." (Numbers 33:52-53)

"But if you do not drive out the inhabitants of the Land before you, those of them who you leave shall be pins in your eyes and thorns in your sides, and they will harass you upon the Land in which you dwell. And it shall be that what I had meant to do to them, I shall do to you." (Numbers 33:55-56)

Based on these words, driving out the inhabitants seemed to be a clear injunction for the Children of Israel. A logical, reasonable person could perhaps say that if the inhabitants were peaceful they could stay, but the text is clear about these particularly hostile nations. Letting such mortal enemies remain would only bring great suffering and pain for Israel. Furthermore, said the Biblical verse, not expelling the enemies of Israel would bring upon Israel the expulsions of its own people (see Chapter Nine).

Within this context, the gravity of Joshua's words on the hills of Shiloh cannot be overstated. The Land of Canaan needed to be rapidly but effectively turned into the Land of Israel and all of the hostile nations currently living in the Land needed to be removed, or at least totally dispossessed of any semblance of sovereignty (political rights), and not only for the purpose of preventing idolatry. The inheritance was for the People of Israel, as promised to the Patriarchs and Matriarchs of Israel, and only they could have any say in the destiny of that inheritance.

"I will establish My covenant as an everlasting covenant between Me and you and your descendants after you for the generations to come...and I will give to you and your descendants the Land of your sojourns, all the Land of Canaan, for an everlasting possession, and I will be their God." (Genesis 17:7-8)

That promise was confirmed several times to Moses and then repeated to Joshua. It was on the basis of that everlasting promise that Joshua spoke to the Children of Israel in Shiloh on that day. This was not a time for indecision and peace negotiations with the

Canaanites. A modern, magnanimous Israeli leader would perhaps suggest that only three of the remaining seven tribes should insist on claiming their inheritance, as a "good-will gesture" to Israel's enemies! Joshua would have none of that. It was a time for Israel to be strong and courageous and act decisively to claim its remaining inheritance in the Land, for only thus would God's name be sanctified in the eyes of the nations. Unfortunately, this was not what happened, and in the succeeding years, the Children of Israel were inconsistent at best in taking possession of the Land. (See Judges 1: 27-33)

The message of Numbers 33 was clear and a lesson for future generations. The failure to trust in the Lord, not acting firmly and decisively against the enemies of God would prove to be the cause of great suffering. This is apparently a shortcoming that Israel suffers from to this day.

The Young Maidens of Shiloh

There is a modern expression that if you ask two Jews a question, you're going to get three different answers. Jews have always been very strong-willed in voicing their opinions and the debates within Israel have been known to be fierce. At the same time, the Jewish people, especially those rooted in their tradition, are particularly sensitive to the dangers of internal conflict. One of the worst cases of inter-tribal conflict and battle in ancient Israel occurred approximately 3,300 years ago after all of the tribes of Israel had confronted the tribe of Benjamin about a horrible act of immorality, sexual abuse, rape, and violence carried out by a group of Benjaminites in Gibeah.

"It happened that whoever saw it said, 'Such a thing has never happened nor been seen since the day the Children of Israel went up from the land of Egypt to this day! You must contemplate this, take counsel, and speak up!'" (Judges 19:30)

The other tribes demanded that the perpetrators be punished, but the Benjaminites refused to deal with the issue. After exhausting all efforts at dialogue, the tribes joined in combat against the tribe of Benjamin, and many thousands were killed on both sides. All of the women and children of Benjamin were killed, and at the end of the war only 600 men remained. (Judges 20)

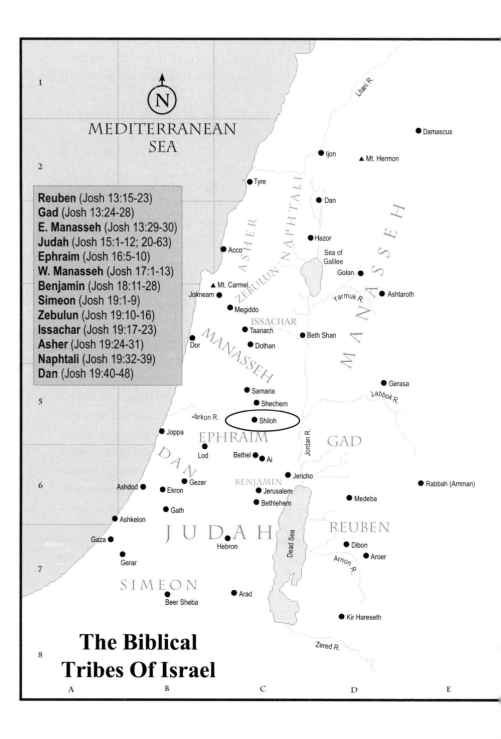

The Biblical Tribes Of Israel

Reuben (Josh 13:15-23)
Gad (Josh 13:24-28)
E. Manasseh (Josh 13:29-30)
Judah (Josh 15:1-12; 20-63)
Ephraim (Josh 16:5-10)
W. Manasseh (Josh 17:1-13)
Benjamin (Josh 18:11-28)
Simeon (Josh 19:1-9)
Zebulun (Josh 19:10-16)
Issachar (Josh 19:17-23)
Asher (Josh 19:24-31)
Naphtali (Josh 19:32-39)
Dan (Josh 19:40-48)

After the war had ended, and the heat of the battle was over, the heavy human cost of the war and the damage to national unity became clearly apparent, and the Children of Israel, feeling the pain of that breach, sought a way to save the tribe of Benjamin from extinction. The problem was clear. The young men of Benjamin would not be able to bring into the world another generation of Benjaminites, so wives had to be found for these young men, or the tribe of Benjamin would cease to exist. The solution, however, was more elusive.

In short, the problem to be solved was not as simple as it seemed. During the war, the People of Israel had taken a vow at Mitzpah that they would not permit their daughters to marry the men of Benjamin. In Judaism, breaking a vow is not such a simple process. Therefore, there would be no way for the men of Benjamin to marry women from the other tribes, or so it seemed.

Fortunately, there were creative thinkers around, and the "solution" was found – to match the 400 young maidens of Jabesh-Gilead with the men of Benjamin, since the men of Jabesh-Gilead had not taken part in the oath. The men of Benjamin appreciated the gesture of peace, but it obviously wasn't enough, since anyone with a basic knowledge of arithmetic knows that 0+400 does not equal 600. Finally, the elders of the tribes came up with an idea through which the vow would not have to be broken, but wives would be found:

"They said, 'Behold, there is a yearly holiday unto the Lord at Shiloh, which is north of Beth El, east of the road going up from Beth El to Shechem, and south of Levonah. So they directed the sons of Benjamin, saying, 'Go and lie in wait in the vineyards. And see; and behold, if the daughters of Shiloh go out to perform the dances, you shall emerge from the vineyards, and each of you grab his wife from the daughters of Shiloh, and go to the land of Benjamin. It shall be that if their fathers or brothers come to protest to us, we will say to them, 'Be compassionate to them (the Benjaminites), for we did not capture a wife for each man in the war (with Jabesh-Gilead), and because you did not give them (the wives) to them, that you should be guilty now.' The sons of Benjamin did so. They took wives according to their number from the dancers, whom they had abducted, and they went and returned to their inheritance; they rebuilt the cities and they settled in them." (Judges 21:19-23)

Thus, the problem was solved. Even though it appears that the "abductions" were consensual, and the dancing young maidens in

47

The Oldest Recorded Singles Gathering: *The beautiful young maidens of Shiloh dance in the vineyards, while the young men of Benjamin watch eagerly, looking for the perfect match. The Hebrew writing reads: Tu B'Av in Shiloh (The 15th day of the month of Av in Shiloh).*

48

their white dresses probably played an active role in the success of this unique singles gathering, the dilemma of the solemn vow was overcome. Since the young maidens of Shiloh were technically "taken," and not "given" by their fathers, no vows had to be broken. Thus, the unity of the people was restored, and the next generations of Benjamin would come to be. This act of national reconciliation through creative thinking stands as a testament to the potential of Shiloh as a catalyst for unity and peace.

To this day, there is a yearly holiday unto the Lord in Shiloh every summer on *Tu B'Av* (the 15th day of the Hebrew month of Av). There are concerts and celebrations and very often gatherings of single men and women who have come to Shiloh searching for their soul mates. The holiday has even spread to other parts of Israel and, although to a lesser extent, to observant Jewish communities around the world. In the more secular circles in Israel, it has become known as "The Holiday of Love," although most who celebrate it are probably unaware of its Biblical roots. Yet for those who know the story of the remaining men from the tribe of Benjamin and their visit to the vineyards of Shiloh, the modern holiday is a reminder of our rich history and the great act of Israel's reconciliation that took place in Shiloh.

The true story of the young maidens of Shiloh has been known by all of the cultures and peoples who have sojourned in the valley of Shiloh through the centuries. The Arabs have always referred to the Shiloh valley as "Marj el-Banat", or "The Valley of the Daughters". In our times, there are once again many vineyards in the valley of Shiloh and the tradition of crushing grapes and making wine has been renewed by the People of Israel who have returned. They have also renewed the tradition of finding a bride from the beautiful young maidens of Shiloh. Indeed, the memories of the past are influencing the present. Yes, in our times as well, those with a minimal imagination can easily visualize the daughters of Shiloh in their white dresses dancing in the vineyards, while the sons of Benjamin lie in wait, hoping to find the perfect match.

"There were no holidays for Israel as joyous as the 15th of Av (Tu B'Av) and Yom HaKippurim" (Talmud: Ta'anit 30b)

I'd like to add to this a short personal note. When I first moved

Hannah's Prayer: A monument commemorating at Tel Shiloh

to Shiloh in 1992, I was thirty-five years old and still single. When I told people that I had decided to move to Shiloh, they responded that I was crazy. What thirty-five year old single in his right mind would move to such a family-oriented community? According to my self-appointed advisors, it would have been better to move to Jerusalem, where all of the religious singles live and congregate. Defying their expectations, after several months of living in Shiloh, I met the beautiful young woman who would soon become my wife. True, she wasn't dancing in the Shiloh vineyards with a white dress on, and she wasn't even wearing a white dress on our first date, but to this day, I'm convinced that it was the merit of Shiloh in bringing single people together that enabled us to meet.

Hannah and Samuel

> "...True prophecy is essentially the flow of thought which descends from God...on the intellect first, and after on the imagination. Prophecy is clearly the highest human level, and the ultimate perfection that may be found in humanity."
>
> *Moses Maimonides*
> *(the Rambam),*
> *The Guide for the Perplexed:*
> *Part 2, Chapter 36)*

From our previous section, we learned about the historic significance of Shiloh in the matchmaking process. As many lonely singles around the world can tell you, it's not easy to find the right man or woman, especially when one waits until a relatively late age to marry. The personals sections in American magazines are filled with hundreds of creative ads attempting to attract Mr. or Ms. Right. There is no doubt that once it finally happens and the happy couple weds, it's very exciting. But the creation of the marriage bond is usually but the first step in the creation of a family. For some the process of conception comes very easily. For many others, it can be a long and stressful ordeal, involving great frustration and disappointment, and often leading to seemingly endless medical consultations and fertility treatments. A simple internet search for the word "infertility" brought up over 25,000 sources of information, which seems to indicate the depths of the problem and the extent of the medical research seeking to meet the public demand for solutions.

The First Book of Samuel begins with a beautiful story of pain and faith that many of these couples would undoubtedly find inspiring. It is also a story about the power of prayer. There was a woman named Hannah who was from a place called Ramah, just north of Jerusalem. She and her husband had been trying, unsuccessfully, to have children. This was a source of great pain for her, especially since her husband Elkanah also had a second wife (which at that time was quite acceptable), and from whom he already did have children. The second wife, recognizing Hannah's vulnerability and showing no sensitivity, provoked her mercilessly. Nonetheless, Elkanah's love for Hannah was much greater than for the second wife. He also felt her grief at her inability to conceive and he didn't hesitate to express his feelings.

"Hannah, why do you cry and why do you not eat? Why is your heart broken? Am I not better to you than ten children?" (1 Samuel 1:8)

Hannah went to the Tabernacle in Shiloh and poured out her soul to the Creator, as Eli the High Priest sat on a chair at the doorpost of the Sanctuary of the Lord:

"She was feeling bitter, and she prayed to the Lord, weeping continuously. She made a vow and said, 'God, Master of Legions, if You take note of the suffering of Your maidservant, and You remember me and do not forget Your maidservant, and give your maidservant a male child, then I shall give him to the Lord all the days of his life, and a razor shall not come upon his head." (1 Samuel 1:9-11)

As Hannah prayed, Eli noticed that her lips were moving, but no sounds were coming out. He couldn't hear any discernible words, so he mistakenly assumed that she was drunk. He strongly reprimanded her for arriving at the Tabernacle in such a condition:

"How long will you be drunk? Remove your wine from yourself!" Hannah answered and said, "No, my lord, I am a woman of aggrieved spirit. I have drunk neither wine nor strong drink, and I have poured out my soul before the Lord. Do not deem your maidservant to be a base woman – for it is out of much grievance and anger that I have spoken until now." Eli, apparently realizing his mistake, answered her, saying, "Go in peace. The God of Israel will grant the request you have made of Him." (1 Samuel 1:14-17)

The request was indeed granted, and Hannah and Elkanah's son was Samuel, the last and the greatest of the Judges and a Prophet of Israel second only to Moses. Hannah, a prophet in her own right with her silent prayer and her lips moving, set the standard for Jewish prayer, which remains the standard to this day. When Jews pray, their lips are always moving, even during the *Shmoneh Esreh*, the silent prayer which forms the basis of the three times daily prayer service. This comes from the woman Hannah and her clear, emotional prayer that she cried out to the Master of the Universe in Shiloh. She kept her promise as well, to give her son to God for service in the Tabernacle in Shiloh. The word Shiloh means "a gift to God" and Samuel the Prophet was, indeed, in the service of the Almighty for the rest of his days.

Hannah raised her son through infancy and his first few years of life, and when she felt he was ready, she brought him back to Shiloh. At this time, she stood before God once again in Shiloh and she once again poured out her soul in the poem of praise to the Almighty that has become known as Hannah's Prayer, regarded by the Torah Sages as one of the great prophetic poems. It recognizes that there are no permanent human conditions in this world, that the Master of the Universe apportions them according to what people and nations need or deserve. It also affirms the power of prayer in influencing the spiritual workings of this world:

"...My heart exults in the Lord, my horn has been raised through the Lord; my mouth is opened wide against my antagonists, for I rejoice in Your salvation. There is none as holy as the Lord, for there is none beside You, and there is no rock like our God. Do not abound in speaking with arrogance upon arrogance, let not haughtiness come from your mouth; for the Lord is a God of knowledge, and by Him actions are weighed. The bow of the mighty is broken, while the foundering are girded with strength. Those who are full and satisfied are hired out for bread, while the hungry ones cease to be so; while the barren woman bears seven (Hannah would eventually have seven), the one with many children becomes bereft. The Lord brings death and gives life, He lowers to the grave and raises up. The Lord impoverishes and makes rich, He humbles and He elevates. He raises the needy from the dirt, from the trash heaps He lifts the destitute, to seat them with nobles and to endow them with a seat of honor, for the pillars of the earth are the Lord's, and upon them He set the world. He guards the steps of His devout ones, but the wicked are stilled in darkness, for not through strength does man prevail. The adversaries of the Lord shall be shattered, let the heavens thunder against them. The Lord will judge to the ends of the earth; He will give strength to His king and raise the pride of His anointed one." (I Samuel 2:1-10)

Hannah thus concludes her prophetic prayer with a blessing for her son, Samuel the Prophet (God's anointed one). Acting through her son Samuel, the Lord did indeed give strength to His kings. The first two kings of Israel, Saul and David, were anointed, advised, and often reprimanded, by Hannah's son, by Samuel the Prophet, who taught them that the true meaning of royalty is to serve their people by serving their Maker.

Normalcy and Tension

The Shiloh period represented a people's struggle for "normalcy" and a natural existence in the Land, but it was also fraught with tension between the tribes of Joseph (as represented through the tribe of his son Ephraim) and Judah. Joseph, while also known for his deep spiritual insights (see the Book of Genesis, Chapters 40-47) was the epitome of active involvement in the material world. He rose to the highest level of government in pre-slavery Egypt through his own hard work and God-given talents, yet he was very connected to the Land of Israel, insisting that he be buried in the Land, in Shechem, about a fifteen minute car ride north of Shiloh. Judah, on the other hand, known for his ability to blend his high level of spirituality with his physical nature, was destined to be the tribe of kingship, as eventually represented by the unified kingdom that was to rise in Jerusalem. Before the entry into the Land after the desert wanderings, there had been tension over who would be Moses' successor, Joshua (from the tribe of Ephraim) or Caleb (from the tribe of Judah). God chose Joshua, perhaps due to the mastery of the physical world so characteristic of the descendants of Joseph, a skill that was apparently just what was needed at that time. Nonetheless, a degree of tension remained between their two tribes, at least until the unification of their two strengths as represented in David and Solomon's unified kingdom in Jerusalem. It's perhaps relevant to point out that the Holy of Holies in the Temple was in the portion of Benjamin, geographically situated between the portions of Ephraim (north of Jerusalem) and Judah (south of Jerusalem). Thus, the tribe of Benjamin which had been the source of such division in the past and had incited the war between itself and the other tribes, eventually merited being a symbol of unity binding together the competing tribes.

Looking back many years prior, the Biblical Joseph (see Genesis 45), had been sold into slavery as a child by his half-brothers, including Judah. Joseph eventually rose to prominence in Egypt and became the governor under Pharaoh. When the brothers came to Egypt, Joseph used his brother Benjamin to attain a sincere reconciliation between him and his half-brothers. There are those who insist that the merit of the original Benjamin ultimately caused his tribe to be the unifying symbol, both geographically and spiritually in the Holy of Holies in the Temple in Jerusalem, thereby bridging the tensions between the competing tribes.

The Tabernacle

As discussed earlier, the Tabernacle (in Hebrew, Mishkan) stood in Shiloh for 369 years. It was the first Permanent Tabernacle, built from stone walls, as opposed to the foldable, portable wooden walls of the wandering Tabernacle of the desert. Shiloh was the first place since the Exodus from Egypt where the Children of Israel said, "That's it. No more running. No more wandering. This is home." The Tabernacle represented that intention of permanence. Its presence in Shiloh made Shiloh the center, to which the Children of Israel would come four times a year to worship God, on the festivals of Sukkot, Passover, Shavuot and Tu B'Av. The dimensions of the Tabernacle are clearly laid out in the Bible, in fulfillment of a central commandment:

"They shall make a Sanctuary for Me, so that I may dwell among them..." (Exodus 25:8)

The great medieval Biblical commentator known as Rashi (Rabbi Shlomo Yitzchaki) emphasized the words, "Sanctuary for Me", and pointed out that the Tabernacle (the Hebrew translation, Mishkan, literally means "the dwelling place") was meant only to be dedicated to God's service. The lesson from this commentary is that no place of worship, no matter how large, grandiose and elegant, is worth anything, if it is not truly dedicated to the Lord's service. Furthermore, the Tabernacle site was to be used only for holiness. No mundane and certainly no immoral behavior was to be permitted at the site.

Rectangular in shape, the Tabernacle consisted of two primary areas: the Holy of Holies and the Tent of Meeting, although the entire Tabernacle itself was occasionally referred to as the Tent of Meeting (see Exodus 40:6-7). Only the High Priest could enter the Holy of Holies, and only on the holiest of days, on Yom Kippur. The Holy of Holies was adjacent to the Holy Place, on its eastern side, separated by a veil. The central feature of the Holy of Holies was the Ark of the Covenant, which was covered with pure gold. It contained the Tablets of the Law. In Hebrew, this was known as the Edut, or Witness, for the Chosen People were to be the Lord's witnesses in this world.

Despite the stone walls of the Tabernacle in Shiloh, which indicate permanence and the development of a more stable existence for the People of Israel, the roof consisted of skins. This was similar to the more temporary dwelling of a tent.

"He abandoned the Tabernacle of Shiloh, the tent where He dwelled among men." (Psalms 78:60)

This alludes to the dual nature of the Tabernacle in Shiloh. Yes, it did establish a degree of permanence after the temporal life in the wilderness, but the tension between Shiloh's nature as a permanent center (as represented by the stone walls) and its transitory nature (as represented by the roof of skins) was ever-present and proved to be prophetic, since Shiloh was eventually destroyed and the capital was eventually re-established in Jerusalem.

It's interesting to take note of the difference between the Ark of the Covenant in the desert and the Ark of the Covenant in Shiloh. The most obvious difference was that of mobility, that the Ark of the desert needed to be carried from place to place, but the key distinction was of a more spiritual nature. In the desert, the Ark of the Covenant, symbolizing God's presence, rested in the very midst of the people. This symbolized the people's dependency on the Holy One's miracles, from the Exodus until the entry into the Land of Israel. These had included the splitting of the Red Sea, the Manna from Heaven, and the raising of the hands of Moses into the air during the battle against the Amalekites.

The establishment of the Tabernacle in Shiloh, and the setting up of the Ark of the Covenant in the Holy of Holies of the Tabernacle, symbolized the beginning of a crucial transitional stage, akin to the necessary stage of human adolescence. In adolescence, we see the transition from childhood to adulthood, from dependency on one's parents, to confusion and exploration and a struggle to "find one's self." This gradually and eventually leads to maturity and independence (even though we all know some adults who never quite reach that stage!).

Likewise, the Children of Israel in the desert had been dependent on God for almost everything, like a young child. They came into the Land and fourteen years later arrived in Shiloh. From the moment that the Tabernacle was established in Shiloh, a new reality set in and the Children of Israel entered their "adolescence" as a people. For 369 years, they struggled with "finding themselves as a people." This included trying to figure out their relationship with their Creator, with their Torah and with each other. The Ark of the Covenant being permanently (at least for now) placed in the Tabernacle in Shiloh, represented that period of adolescence. No longer would the Ark follow them (and symbolically hold their hands) wherever they would go. The people needed to learn to be mature functioning adults in the Land of Israel – growing their own crops, building their own army, and creating a national economy. No longer could they rely on God's overt miracles to take care of them every step of the way. Just as parents need to raise up their children through adolescence by helping them to become independent, so too, God, acting through Samuel the Prophet, enabled the Children of Israel to grow up as a nation.

One symbolic manifestation of this healthy, but often uncomfortable tension was the eating of the sacrifices that had been performed in the Tabernacle. After the sacrifices were performed in the Tabernacle of the desert, the people were required to eat them within the camp. In contrast to this, the Talmud (Zevachim 118) refers to the fact that people were permitted to eat the sacrifices of Shiloh anywhere outside the city walls as long as they were able to see Shiloh from where they were eating. It reminds me of the familiar anecdote of children who are walking to someplace with their parents and want to run ahead, as far ahead as they can. The usual parental response is, "Okay, as long as you don't run ahead so far that you can't see us." Just as there are those periods of healthy tension between parents and children seeking autonomy, so too the time that the Tabernacle stood in Shiloh was a period of tentative steps towards maturity and independence for the Children of Israel. Through this period, which turned out to be an often difficult period of painful growth as a people, the Children of Israel learned to be the People of Israel, with the goal of being responsible adults, who would have the potential of creating a unified, prosperous kingdom that would be a Sanctification of God's Name. That was the role of Samuel the Prophet, to guide Israel to the next stage.

Samuel himself grew up into adolescence in Shiloh during this period of greatness, mixed with turmoil and division. So, too his role in raising up His People. Samuel the Prophet, who himself epitomized that growth to adulthood and maturity, was destined to lead the Children of Israel through adolescence into adulthood, by taking the necessary steps that would lead to the unified Kingdom of Israel and the building of the Holy Temple in Jerusalem.

The Destruction of Shiloh

Throughout Jewish history, we read about miracles and tragedy, very often occurring one after the other. Shiloh was no exception to this pattern. Samuel the Prophet's birth to the seemingly barren woman Hannah and her husband Elkanah was the result of his mother's prayers in Shiloh, prayers which to this day serve as a model of how to relate to the Creator. After a brief childhood, Samuel quickly entered the Lord's service in Shiloh and became God's spokesman during one of the most difficult periods of Israel's growth. Such spiritual loftiness, most people can only dream of. Just imagine, God speaking to His Chosen People through you! However, despite the glory, despite the stability, despite the immense spirituality of the Tabernacle in Shiloh, the prophet would soon be forced to deliver a message to Eli the High Priest that was not so pleasant, that in fact foretold that the days of glory for Shiloh would soon be coming to an end. It was also a message that hit very close to home for Eli, for the coming destruction of Shiloh would be due to the terrible sins of his two sons, Hophni and Pinchas, who officiated in the Tabernacle in Shiloh, but abused their positions of authority, simultaneously committing grave sins of morality.

"Eli became very old. He heard about all that his sons were doing to all of Israel, and that they would lie with the women who congregated at the entrance of the Tent of Meeting..." (1 Samuel 2:22-23)

Most people would agree that with leadership comes an obligation to be a moral example, although many voters will look the other way and ignore acts of corruption and sexual immorality carried out by politicians, if it serves their perceived interests. As we well know, there have been many cases of sexual immorality by both political and religious leaders. The story of Hophni and Pinchas makes it clear that the spiritual leader has an even greater responsibility to serve as a moral example. This certainly is not meant to excuse the political leaders who are unfaithful to their wives or lie in a court of law, rather to stress that one who claims to be a spiritual leader and uses the title of Pastor or Father or Rabbi or any other religious title, has a greater moral responsibility to lead by example. In addition, Eli's failure to take decisive action and God's instructive response emphasizes that one who looks the other way because of the lack of public uproar can be culpable as well, even though he wasn't directly responsible for what occurred.

"The Lord said to Samuel, 'Behold, I am going to do (such) a thing in Israel that when anyone hears about it, both of his ears will ring. On that day, I will fulfill for Eli all that I have spoken concerning his house, from beginning to end. I have told him that I am executing judgment against his house forever for the sin (he committed) that he was aware that his sons were blaspheming, and he didn't restrain them." (1 Samuel 3:11-13)

That day eventually came, and Israel went out to war against their bitter enemy, the Philistines. The battle took place in the fields of Even HaEzer, near what is today called Rosh Ha'Ayin, in modern terms about a thirty minute drive from Shiloh, but in those days it was quite a journey. The Philistines were easily victorious in the opening battle, killing four thousand soldiers of Israel.

"The people came to the camp, and the elders of Israel said, 'Why did the Lord smite us today before the Philistines? Let us take with us from Shiloh the Ark of the Covenant of the Lord, that when it comes among us, it will save us from the hands of our enemies!" (1 Samuel 4:3)

Both Samuel and Eli objected to removing the Ark from the Tabernacle in Shiloh, asserting that to use the Ark of the Covenant as an object with magical powers was akin to idolatry. When the ark had been taken to war in the time of Joshua, it had been a result of God's clear instructions, unlike in the present situation. The protests of Samuel the Prophet and Eli the High Priest were ignored, and the warriors rushed to the battlefront, in their possession the Ark, which they had forcibly removed from its resting place. At first, the Philistines were afraid, but they quickly regrouped and soundly defeated the fighters of Israel, killing thirty thousand foot soldiers. Eli's sons

Hophni and Pinchas were among the fallen in battle. The Bible tells the story of the man from the tribe of Benjamin who came running to Shiloh, a messenger from the battlefront, with ripped clothing and dirt upon his head. He approached Eli, who was then ninety-eight years old and blind, waiting anxiously near the gate to the city:

"The messenger answered him (Eli), saying, 'Israel ran from before the Philistines; and there was a great blow among the people; also, your two sons Hophni and Pinchas died; and the Ark of the Lord was taken!' As soon as he (the messenger) mentioned the Ark of the Lord, (Eli) collapsed backwards off his chair, opposite the city gate, breaking his neck and he died, for the man was old and heavy. He had judged Israel for forty years." (1 Samuel 4:17-18)

The Philistines soon marched on to Shiloh, setting the city aflame and causing great destruction. It would take 52 years from the time of the destruction until the Tabernacle was once again in a stable, permanent setting. How can we understand the destruction, and more specifically, the failure of the presence of the Ark to save Israel in its fateful battle against the Philistines? After all, the Ark of the Covenant stood in the midst of the Children of Israel in the desert encampments, with the cloud, representing God's presence, hovering above it. When they went out to battle they took the Ark with them. Even after entering the Land, in Jericho, the Ark played a pivotal role in the conquest. Why not in the battle against the Philistines at Even HaEzer? As we discussed earlier in this chapter, the role of the Ark of the Covenant changed as did the relationship between the Children of Israel and their Creator. Even when the Children of Israel were in the desert, at their most dependent state, the Ark was just a representation of God's presence, meant to remind them that their ability to succeed in battle was dependent on His will and the people's adherence to His commandments.

"And you may say in your heart, 'My strength and the might of my hand made me all this wealth!' Then you shall remember the Lord, your God, that it was He Who gave you strength..." (Deuteronomy 8:17-18)

The Ark of the Covenant was used by God to remind the Children of Israel of His presence, not to be used by the people as a tool of battle. By deciding on their own to use the Ark itself almost as a weapon, the People of Israel were crossing the line between using the Ark of the Covenant as a reminder that the Lord is with them, and actually believing in an object and its "magical powers", rather than in God Himself. As we discussed earlier, this could be considered idolatry. Thus, they were coming dangerously close to imitating their Philistine enemies, for whom idolatry was a way of life. We should also take note of the excessive individualism and even rebelliousness during much of the Shiloh period, which, as we discussed earlier, represented a period of adolescence for the People of Israel. Just as adolescents are often known to be great idealists and spiritual seekers, they also tend to have very strong opinions and a rebellious nature. The insistence on taking the Ark out to battle, despite the objections of Eli and Samuel seemed to fit this blend of idealism and rebellion.

Psychologists and educators have often pointed out the adolescent potential for great passion and achievement, with the flip side of the coin being the potential for great argumentativeness and even seriously destructive behavior.

"In those days there was no king in Israel; every man did that which seemed proper in his own eyes." (Judges 21:25)

While the end result of this excessive individualism and rebelliousness in ancient Shiloh was great destruction, the adolescent potential for greatness lived on in Samuel the Prophet. This young man, born from the merit of his mother's prayers in the Tabernacle of Shiloh, who had literally grown up in Shiloh, physically, emotionally, and spiritually, would soon lead His People into the greatest era of all, the unified Kingdom of Israel.

Chapter Four

From Kings To Exiles

"What an amazing coincidence!"
"What an astonishing fit of nature!"
"Weren't you lucky!"

Such expressions are often heard in everyday conversations between people in all walks of life, but for the Jew, and indeed, for any person who believes in the God of Israel, these expressions are misguided at best. Why is that so? For the simple reason that this world has an omnipotent Creator, who created an amazing system of nature and life, and the spiritual forces of good and evil. There are no mere coincidences, nature operates according to guidelines created by the Master of the Universe, and things don't just occur by chance. It's as if we were witnessing one gigantic subway system. Generally, things operate routinely and people don't think about whether their train will reach its destination. However, accidents do happen as a result of human error and mistakes are made, for even though the chief engineer created a remarkable subway system, there is always the potential for human error. This is also true in the greater picture of God's universe. People do have free choice, even if the Almighty knows in advance what those choices will be. Even so, the question is often asked, "Why is there evil in the world?" In fact, while it may be upsetting at times, it really is not an unresolvable existential dilemma for one who believes in God and the wisdom of His Word.

Rabbi Joseph Soloveitchik, of blessed memory, refers to two levels of Divine punishment, known as *Middat Hadin* (Measure for Measure punishment, commensurate with one's sins) and *Hester Panim* (The Hiding of God's Face).

While Measure for Measure demonstrates God's active involvement, The Hiding of the Face describes a temporary suspension of God's active surveillance. Because of the spiritual ramifications of our negative actions, He turns His back, so to speak, on events and leaves matters to chance. When this occurs, all havoc can break loose, as Israel and the world are left to their own devices. This is the worst state of affairs, since humankind hasn't proven itself to be capable of consistently managing on its own.

"Then my anger will flare up against them in that day and I will abandon them and hide My face from them, and they shall be devoured and many evils and distress shall befall them; so that they will say in that day, 'Are not these evils come upon us, because our God is not in our midst?'" *(Deuteronomy 31:17)*

"*Hester Panim* (the hiding of the Face), the Torah indicates, is related to Israel's waywardness and may be regarded as an ultimate punishment. It is terrifying because it signifies rejection. A child can bear a father's reprimand or punishment stoically, but to be totally ignored and treated as persona non grata in one's own home is a frightening experience."
(Reflections of the Rav, p.36)

Yet Israel does possess the potential to avoid that spiritual void by fulfilling its God-given role in this world. As it says in the second chapter of the Book of Genesis:

"By the seventh day, God completed His work which He had done, and He abstained on the seventh day from all His work which He had done. God blessed the seventh day and sanctified it because on it He abstained from all His work which God created to make." (Genesis 2:2-3)

Rabbi Soloveitchik raises the question of the seemingly redundant expression "to make" at the end of the verse. His answer speaks volumes about our purpose in this world and explaining the existence of evil. Our purpose in this world is to complete the creation that the Lord began. That is the meaning of the word "la'asot" in the original Hebrew, which means "to make" or "to do." We were meant to be idealists, to constantly be striving to improve ourselves and to create a better world, indeed to be God's partners in the completion of the Creation. The Almighty intentionally did not create a perfect universe, although astronomers are often amazed when contemplating the complexity of the universe, as are many doctors in awe when seeing the workings of each part of the human body.

"When I behold Your heavens, the work of Your fingers, the moon and the stars that you have set in place; What is man, that You are mindful of him...? Yet You have made him but slightly lower than the angels, and have crowned him with glory and honor." (Psalms 8:4-7)

Our primary task in this world is to reveal both the existing goodness and potential for goodness and beauty in this world that God has created for us to complete. This job of Creation Completion and turning back the forces of evil in the world is set before all of us, but for the People of Israel the responsibility is much greater.

While that role has been taken very seriously by the People of Israel as a whole for several thousand years, the natural Jewish idealism and yearning for completing the creation has in modern times very often been disconnected from the Creator. So many Jews in modern history have put their spiritual energies and brilliance into improving the world in ways that often fall out of the context of Israel's mission in this world. Karl Marx and some of the leaders of the Bolshevik (Communist) Revolution were prime examples of this. Yes, it is very characteristic of the People of Israel to want to improve the world, but it needs to be done in ways that are consistent with, or at least not in conflict with, Israel's divine purpose in this world. Albert Einstein and the long and remarkable list of Jewish Nobel Prize winners are certainly good examples of potentially positive use of that spiritual energy.

"And now, if you will obey My voice and keep My covenant, you shall be to Me the most beloved treasure of all peoples, for Mine is the entire world. You shall be to Me a kingdom of ministers and a holy nation." (Exodus 19:5-6)

There is no escaping this lofty challenge! Despite the stated desire of many Israeli politicians and a large portion of the Israeli populace to "normalize" our existence, Israel wasn't meant to be a nation like all the other nations. Like it or not, Israel is destined to be the vehicle for the sanctification of God's Name in this world, and because of that, our responsibility is that much greater.

What about the other peoples in the world? What should their role be in relation to Israel? For them, the answer is also quite clear: The responsibility of the other nations in the world is to support and encourage the nation of Israel in its God-given role to be "a light unto the nations and the witnesses of the Holy One's presence in this world."

"The degradation of Israel is the desecration of the Name of God."
(Biblical Commentator Rashi's commentary on Ezekiel 39:7)

As the above quote implies, if the Gentile world isn't supportive of Israel's difficult responsibility, and even persecutes God's chosen people, then there are spiritual ramifications for that as well, since that is contrary to God's plan.

If so, then the converse is obviously true as well, that the raising up and glorification of Israel as God's chosen people is a sanctification of God's Name. Urging Israel to be faithful to its heritage and helping Israel to carry out its proper role and responsibility is one important way of bringing **genuine normalcy** to the world.

This brings us to the period of the unified Kingdom of Israel in Jerusalem, which represents the apex of the glorification of Israel, hence the sanctification of God's Name. As we discussed earlier, Samuel the Prophet's primary role was to guide His People from its adolescence, which entailed excessive individualism and lack of unity during the period of the Judges, to maturity and unity in the unified kingdom that was later established in Jerusalem. Samuel anointed Saul as king during the post-Shiloh pre-Jerusalem period, the 52 years during which the Ark of the Covenant was in limbo, as was the stability of the nation. The Philistines had taken the Ark after destroying Shiloh and it was eventually returned to Israel and brought to Jerusalem by King David, who also had been anointed by Samuel. The kings of Israel had been anointed as a result of popular demand, sort of a modified expression of democracy in favor of a modified version of monarchy. After the long period of division, excessive individualism, and lack of leadership in Israel during the Judges period, the people wanted one strong leader who would really take charge. Speaking through Samuel, the Master of the Universe had warned the people of the potential abuse of power that was commonplace among monarchies in the world. He stressed that the system was no panacea for their problems, but the people were not dissuaded.

"But the people refused to listen to the voice of Samuel. They said, 'No! There shall be a king over us, and we will be like all the other nations; our king will judge us, and go forth before us, and fight our wars!" (1 Samuel 8:19-20)

Samuel, on the other hand, tried to convey the message of the perils of monarchy without limits, pointing out that just having a strong leader was playing with fire. In fact, it could be very dangerous to put unlimited power in the hands of one person. While it was good to have a strong leader, only one who would be subservient to the will of God, would be successful in leading the nation forward in strength and unity. Recognizing that his previous warning wasn't enough to persuade the people, he later tried again.

"And now, here is the king whom you have chosen, whom you have requested; and behold, God has set a king over you. If you will fear the Lord and worship Him and hearken to His voice and not rebel against the word of the Lord, then you and the king who reigns over you will be following the Lord your God. But if you do not hearken to the voice of the Lord, and you rebel against the word of the Lord, then the hand of the Lord will be against you, and against your fathers." (1 Samuel 12:13-15)

The Biblical commentator known as the Radak said that the words "your fathers" in the quote refers to the kings. In other words, Samuel is giving a very clear warning and prophecy that the kings were required at least as much as all of the people, to adhere to God's Torah. For that reason, the ruler was required, immediately upon taking office, to write his own Torah scroll. This would make it clear to all exactly Who was actually on the throne. Thus, Samuel wisely took the desire of the people and crafted it according to the Divine will, thereby creating a sort of democracy/monarchy that would ideally be subservient to God's Plan. The king, appointed due to the demand of the people, would know his role, and more importantly, the limits of his power.

King Saul, the first king of Israel, failed to achieve that ideal, ignoring the Almighty's explicit instructions to destroy the entire nation of Amalek, including their livestock. Instead, he allowed the people to take sheep and cattle from the spoils. King Saul then tried to rationalize his lack of obedience to God's explicit instructions, saying that they were planning to sacrifice the animals to give offerings to the

Lord, but Samuel would hear none of it.

"Does God delight in elevation-offerings and feast-offerings, as in obedience to the voice of the Lord? Behold! To obey is better than a choice offering, to be attentive than the fat of rams. For rebelliousness is like the sin of sorcery, and verbosity is like the iniquity of idolatry. Because you have rejected the word of God, he has rejected you as king!" *(I Samuel 15:22-23)*

Samuel removed Saul from his position, and following God's instructions, anointed David as king. This handsome young man from Bethlehem became known as the "sweet singer of Israel": the accomplished musician, who played beautiful music on his harp; the poet, who wrote the hundreds of psalms of praise to the Almighty that continue to be recited to this day; and the warrior, who boldly led Israel into battle against its enemies.

"Halleluyah! Praise the Lord in His Sanctuary; praise Him in the firmament of His power; praise Him for His mighty acts; praise Him as befits His abundant greatness; praise Him with the blast of the shofar; praise Him with lyre and harp; praise Him with drum and dance; praise Him with organ and flute; praise Him with clanging cymbals; praise Him with resonant trumpets. Let all souls praise God. Halleluyah!" *(Psalms 150:1-6)*

King David was the prototype of what the Israeli leader should be, in touch with all realms of spirituality, but also very much the strong military leader. Both of those elements were needed to create and maintain the unified Kingdom of Israel. David understood and epitomized that concept of Jewish kingship and leadership. That is not to say that he was perfect. Like anyone, he had his human flaws, which he was punished for, but he recognized his mistakes and never once doubted the authority of God's Torah.

David understood, as well, that there could be no legitimate kingship without the Holy Temple in Jerusalem. The primary role of the king was to show the world that God is the real King. The Temple was to be located on Mt. Moriah. This was the same place where hundreds of years earlier, the Patriarch Abraham, the first Jew, had been given his ultimate test of faith. God had commanded him to sacrifice his only son, Isaac. Abraham was about to carry out the act when the Creator stopped him. Abraham had passed the test with flying colors and the prophecy for his descendants was revealed.

"The angel of God called to Abraham a second time from heaven. And he said, 'By myself I swear, the word of the Lord, that because you have done this thing, and have not withheld your son, your only one, that I shall surely bless you and increase your offspring like the stars of the heavens and like the sand on the seashore; and your offspring shall inherit the gate of its enemy, And all the nations shall bless themselves by your offspring, because you have listened to My voice.'" (Genesis 22:15-18)

On this exact location, the Holy Temple would be built, but the Almighty had already decided that King David would not be the one to do it.

"He summoned his son Solomon and commanded him to build a Temple for the Lord, God of Israel. David said to Solomon, 'My son, I had in mind to build a Temple for the Name of the Lord my God, but the word of the Lord came to me saying, 'You have shed much blood and have made great wars; you shall not build a Temple for My Name's sake, for you have shed much blood upon the ground before Me." (Chronicles 22:6-8)

The Temple symbolized the perfect, ideal world that the Almighty wished for us to bring to fruition. Although war against evildoers was certainly justified, war and bloodshed had no place in the ideal world of the Temple, and David had been involved in many wars in his day. Solomon, on the other hand, had inherited the already unified and sovereign kingdom from David, so didn't need to engage in war on the scale that David needed to. David set the stage for the building of the Temple. Solomon's role was to see it to fruition.

David's role in this case was that of an enabler. Just as Samuel the Prophet brought up Israel to Kingship, David brought Israel up to Templeship, but Solomon carried it out. At the same time, it's important to remember that God was by no means reprimanding David for the blood of Israel's enemies that had been shed. The proof of this is that David purchased the Temple Mount, prepared the site (Chronicles 21), and the Messiah who the prophets have told us will build the Third Temple in Jerusalem, is referred to as coming from the ancestral lineage of David.

David's Kingdom of Israel had lasted for 40 years, and he passed the mantle to his son, Solomon, a man of peace and great wisdom, who, as we've discussed, merited building the Holy Temple. King Solomon also sat on the throne for 40 years, but his Kingdom came to an abrupt end due to idolatrous worship, that he had allowed and even enabled and supported.

"King Solomon loved many foreign women, in addition to the daughter of Pharaoh, Moabite, Ammonite, Edomite, Sidonian, and Hittite women, from the nations concerning whom the Lord said to the Children of Israel, 'Do not go into them and they shall not come into you, for they will surely sway your hearts after their gods.' Solomon clung to them for love... So it was that when Solomon grew old, his wives swayed his heart after the gods of others, and his heart was not as complete with the Lord his God as had been the heart of his father David." (1 Kings 11:1-2, 4)

The Torah had warned the future kings of Israel, many years prior to their anointing (Deuteronomy 17:16-17), that the king should not have too many wives (even though polygamy was, at least in theory, permitted in those days). The stated reason for God's objection to Solomon's excessively active love life was that his heart would be led astray, which is what actually happened. He was also warned not to have too many horses, so that he wouldn't be tempted to have a close relationship with Egypt, which bred the finest horses. Solomon apparently thought that his great wisdom would help him to overcome these very human temptations, but he was clearly mistaken, since God's understanding of human nature was obviously far greater than the intellect of any human.

After the fall of Solomon's kingdom and his death, the kingdom split in two, into the kingdoms of Israel and Judah. For the next 300 plus years, an assortment of kings ruled over Israel and Judah, some more distinguished than others, but the glory of the unified kingdom never returned. In the year 722 B.C.E., the Assyrian king invaded the Kingdom of Israel, capturing all of Samaria and exiling ten of the twelve tribes of Israel to Assyria. This massive exile included all of the tribes, except for Judah and Benjamin, who comprised the Judean kingdom, to the south. To this day, the whereabouts of most of the ten lost tribes are still unknown, although there are some notable exceptions and in recent years there has been much talk and efforts expended in locating and identifying the descendants of the lost tribes, some reputed to be living distinctive lives as a group and observing Jewish traditions that have been passed down from generation to generation.

"...Thus said the Lord, "If you do not listen to me, to follow my Torah that I have placed before you, to listen to the words of My servants the prophets whom I send to you...I shall make this Temple like Shiloh, and I will make this city (Jerusalem) a curse for all the nations of the land." (Jeremiah 26:4-6)

The Prophet Jeremiah had delivered the warning that the fate of the Temple in Jerusalem would be like that of the Tabernacle in Shiloh, and the destruction was not long in coming. Just 136 years after the first exile, in the year 586 B.C.E., the Temple in Jerusalem was destroyed by the armies of Nebuchadnezzar, the king of Babylonia, and the Kingdom of Judah was destroyed, with substantial numbers of Jews, especially the political and spiritual leaders, exiled to Babylonia.

As we have made clear from the previous chapters, it is nearly impossible for a Jew who is true to his heritage to be an atheist. Yes, we are very aware of the enemies who have brutally oppressed our people and caused great destruction, but the nation of Israel was not formed because of human oppression, but rather in spite of it. We do not excuse that oppression in the least. Nonetheless, being very much an introspective people, we understand that there are spiritual ramifications, not just for our actions as individuals, but for every action taken by the nation of Israel. The Torah Sages of Israel ascribed the destruction of the Temple and the first exile to the idolatry that had been increasingly brought into the Temple worship, and into the overall life of the people, in both kingdoms. These painful events, and the idolatry that was believed to be the cause, were to serve as an important lesson to be learned for the future, a lesson that has been well heeded by the People of Israel to this day. In our times, observant Jews are very wary of anything that might resemble idol worship in any way, shape, or form.

"The Lord had issued a warning in Israel and in Judah through the hand of all prophets of any vision, saying, 'Repent from your evil ways, and observe My commandments and My decrees in accordance with the

entire Torah that I commanded your forefathers, and that I have sent you through My servants the prophets.'" (2 Kings 17:13-14)

The First Exile was to last seventy years. Many of the Jews who had been exiled to Babylonia assimilated into the societies in which they dwelled and never returned, but others returned and rebuilt the Temple, completing the work in 349 B.C.E. The Second Temple was often known as the Temple of Ezra and Nehemiah, who were the prophets of that era. There were some great successes during that time, especially the abolishment of the intense craving for idolatry, an achievement that resonates to this day. During this period as well, Ezra and Nehemiah composed many of the standardized prayers that Jews have continued to recite through the centuries. They also increased and strengthened the teaching of the Oral Law, which had been passed down through the generations from Moses on Mount Sinai. But despite all of these accomplishments, the Second Temple period could never attain the level of holiness of the First Temple. For one thing, there was no genuine political sovereignty for the nation of Israel in its own Land. It was only due to the benevolence of the Persian ruler King Cyrus (part of the Babylonian Empire) that the Temple was allowed to be rebuilt. In a sense, it was almost a continuation of the exile, since Israel was dependent on the kindness of the ruling nation, just the opposite of independence.

"Thus said Cyrus king of Persia, 'All of the kingdoms of the earth has the Lord, God of heaven, given to me and He has commanded me to build Him a Temple in Jerusalem, which is in Judah. Whoever is among you of His entire people, may God be with him, and let him go up to Jerusalem which is in Judah and build the Temple of the Lord, God of Israel – He is the God! – which is in Jerusalem." (Ezra 1:2-3)

The Second Temple period was also a time of great division, rivalries, and even hatred among the People of Israel. This Chosen People, who had risen from their adolescence and growing pains as the Children of Israel in Shiloh to maturity and the glory of David's Kingdom, sunk back to the most destructive levels of immaturity and divisiveness, which would insure the eventual destruction of the Second Temple, and the second and far longer exile from the Land of Israel. In the year 70 C.E., after a long period of Roman rule, the

Temple was destroyed and the city of Jerusalem along with it.

Thus began the long and bitter exile from the Land of Israel. The People of Israel, who would gradually become known more and more, simply as Jews, were scattered around the world. Despite the cruelty of the Romans, who forcibly exiled the Jews from their Land, many Jews viewed the exile as but a natural result of the Lord's people not following His Torah. The Jews were to suffer from nearly two thousand years of persecution, assimilation, and mass murder by many enemies in many lands. Meanwhile, the Romans changed the name of the Land of Israel to Palestina, choosing a Roman variation of the word Philistine, after the long-time arch-enemy of Israel. Clearly, they were attempting to erase the Jewish presence by rewriting the geography and attempting to hide the history of the region. In time, the name of the Land became known to most people as Palestine, to the extent that the Arabs living in the Land of Israel today claim that they are the "indigenous Palestinian people", whatever that means.

There was then and continues to be, however, one people that, thank God, was never fooled by this great historical deception. As the Muslims of Jerusalem prayed with their bodies turned in the direction of Mecca in Saudi Arabia (and with their backs to Jerusalem), the Jewish people always prayed three times a day facing the Land of Israel, and when in Israel, facing the Temple Mount in Jerusalem. The Jews in Spain or Russia, England or Yemen all read daily prayers throughout the winter for rain to fall in the Land of Israel. They continued to read and study books written by the Sages of Israel, which spoke about the holiness of the Land of Israel, and they continued to celebrate the same holidays, observing customs which were integrally tied to the supreme importance of the Land of Israel and the great civilization that had been lost. For a Jew could not be complete as a Jew without the connection to his Land.

"Have pity on us, O Lord, in the land of our captivity, and do not pour Your wrath upon us – for we are Your people, the members of Your covenant." (From the Tachanun prayer)

"Blow the great shofar (ram's horn) for our liberty, and miraculously ingather our exiles, and gather us together from the four corners of the earth. Blessed are You O Lord, who ingathers the dispersed of His People Israel." (From the thrice daily Amidah prayer)

Chapter Five
From Exiles To Zionism

"The farther we went the hotter the sun got, and the more rocky and bare, repulsive and dreary the landscape became...There was hardly a tree or shrub anywhere. Even the olive and the cactus, those fast friends of a worthless soil, had almost deserted the country."

(Mark Twain: on his visit to the Land of Israel, 1867)

The Land Without Its People

The bond between the Jewish people and its Land is of such a spiritual-physical nature that without the presence of its people, the Land couldn't give of its fruit and potential bounty. The Land "flowing with milk and honey" was no longer receiving its necessary spiritual nourishment from the presence of God's Chosen People. This symbiotic relationship between People and Land cannot be emphasized enough. During the almost 2,000 years of foreign occupation, many different populations passed through, often setting up residence and purchasing property, but the Land became a barren wasteland, with group after group fighting over control of the Land. These included the Muslims, the Christian Crusaders, the Ottoman Turks, and eventually the British. There was always a smattering of Jews, concentrated in a few specific places in the Land, such as Jerusalem and a few other holy cities (or former cities), but they frequently lived on charity and often in fear of attack. Only when its people were home as a sovereign, flourishing nation, had the land grown and prospered. The invading nations only brought destruction and death.

"I will make the land desolate; and your foes that dwell upon it will be desolate." (Leviticus 26:32)

Some years after the destruction of Shiloh, Jewish settlement was renewed in the former home of Samuel the Prophet. This remained the situation during the First and Second Temple eras. While I haven't found any specific record of Jewish inhabitants in Shiloh after the Second Temple era, it is reported that the area was populated until the late Middle Ages. In addition, it's clear that there was a steady custom in the 12th and early 13th century of Jews making pilgrimages to the ancient site of the Tabernacle in Shiloh (Past and Remains, Yosef Braslevsky, Pp.299-303). Given the turmoil in the Land of Israel during the time of the Crusades, it's quite remarkable that these pilgrimages actually took place, and on a regular basis.

In fact, a story is told about the Crusaders invading a part of the then populated area of Shiloh as part of their widespread invasions in the 13th century. The French knight, Raymond de St. Gilles, the fourth Count of Toulouse, led a brutal massacre of all the residents of the area, leaving behind some Christian families, building his castle there, and naming the village after himself. (The Survey of Western Palestine: Volume Two, Conder and Kitchener, 1882) Much has changed since then as a result of subsequent Muslim invasions. Today, Sinjil, a predominantly Muslim Arab village, geographically situated very close to Shiloh, and not exactly a friend of Israel or the United States, is said to have been the former home of the infamous Sirhan Sirhan, the assassin of United States Senator Robert F. Kennedy. The base of the mosque in Sinjil is the same base that once supported the Crusader leader's castle in the town. And so it was, all through the 2,000 years of Israel's absence from the Land. The invaders arrived, with a lot of noise and a lot of proclamations, causing great death and bloodshed in their conquests, stayed for some time, and eventually were driven out by the next invaders. Although the Land of Israel was populated at various times, no people succeeded in making the desert bloom, or in planting permanent roots in the land, then known as Palestine.

> *"...the land is left void and desolate and without inhabitants."*
> *(Rev. Samuel Manning, Those Holy Fields, 1874)*

The land was dormant and lonely, as an abandoned mother, as the Matriarch Rachel, waiting for her children to return.

"Thus said the Lord: "A voice is heard on high, wailing, bitter weeping. Rachel weeps for her children; she refuses to be consoled for her children, for they are gone." (Jeremiah 31:14)

The People Without Its Land

If it is true that the Land of Israel without its People is like roots without fertilizer, it is certainly of equal veracity to say that the People of Israel outside the Land of Israel is like a tree without roots, or a fish out of water. A nation is generally bound to its land. That is usually from where its culture derives, its religious customs develop and its style of living evolves. For the Jew, it was true tenfold, for his entire being was inextricably linked with the Land of Israel. For thousands of years, his entire essence was integrated with the Land of Israel and his global, universal mission was intended to be carried out from there, as the Lord first proclaimed to the first Israelite, Abraham, the first believer in the one God.

"The Lord said to Abram, 'Go forth from your land, from your relatives, and from your father's house to the Land that I will show you. And I will make of you a great nation; I will bless you and make your name great, and you shall be a blessing. I will bless those who bless you, and him who curses you I will curse; and all the families of the earth shall bless themselves through you." (Genesis 12:1-3)

Israel's mission as a spiritual light unto the nations couldn't possibly be fulfilled as an oppressed minority in other people's lands. The Jew as a persecuted minority was for the Anti-Semites evidence of God's non-existence, and therefore, a desecration of God's Name. This was the polar opposite of Israel's mission, to bear witness to God's existence, to encourage the world to sing His praises, to encourage all of Israel to follow His commandments, and to sanctify His Name.

"These words which I command you this day shall be upon your heart. You shall teach them diligently to your children, and you shall speak of them while you sit at home, while you walk in the street, while you are lying down, and getting up. Bind them for a sign upon your arm and let them be ornaments between your eyes. And write them upon the doorposts of your house and upon your gates." (Deuteronomy 6:6-8)

"Why should the nations say, 'Where is their God?' Let there be known among the nations, before our eyes, revenge for your servant's spilled blood." (Psalms 79:10)

King David in his Psalms had often referred to Israel as God's servant. When God's servant was persecuted, the existence of the God of Israel was questioned by those who oppressed Israel. These verses became very meaningful during the painful years of exile from the Land.

That isn't to say that there weren't many positive aspects to the sojourn among the nations of the world. The first and foremost was the writing down of the Talmud (the codification of the Oral Torah), which up to that time had been passed down orally from generation to generation from Moses to Joshua and onwards. While there were many reasons for it not having been written down up to that point, the great scholar known as Rabbi Yehuda the Prince foresaw the oncoming exile and recognized the danger that the oral tradition could be lost once the nation was scattered. He immediately got to work writing down the Mishna, and thus began the long process that would take several hundred years, with the end result being the Talmud, which contains a wealth of rabbinical wisdom and Jewish legal discourse compiled over the ages, and comprises the basis for Jewish religious observance in our times. Much of the Talmud was derived from lengthy discussions about the Oral Torah carried out by the Jewish Sages who lived in Babylonia and other countries in the Diaspora.

Spain and Europe

Every American child learns about the great event that occurred in 1492. However, most Americans are unaware that the great discoveries of Christopher Columbus were not the only noteworthy events in that year. It was also the year that the edict was handed down ordering the expulsion of the Jews from Spain. Thus came to an end what had been known as the Golden Age of Spain, but the sojourn in Spain had certainly been a mixed blessing. There had been great Jewish scholarship in Spain, in the realms of Talmudic analysis, Biblical commentary, religious poetry, philosophy, and literature, and Hebrew language. To this day, the works of the Rambam, Ramban, Yehuda Halevi, and others are studied in Jewish schools throughout the world.

In addition, many Jews achieved levels of great prominence in the broader society. Nonetheless, the years in Spain were filled with great oppression, as Jews were forced to undergo periods of forced conversions to Christianity. The often mass violence combined with threats of expulsion to keep the Jews on edge. These methods actually were already reported in the 4th century Frankish kingdoms, but continued, and were quite widespread already in 7th century Spain. These practices continued intermittently in the several hundred years that followed, at various times in other European countries as well. Jews often "went underground", pretending to convert to Catholicism, publicly observing its precepts, but secretly practicing Judaism. These people were known as Marranos, while in Hebrew, they are known as the Anusim (lit., those who were forced against their will). And so it was for Spanish and much of European Jewry. When the pressure of forced conversions and expulsion was on, the Jews often pretended to convert and hid their Judaism in order to assimilate into, and to succeed in, the greater society, or they really converted. When the oppression subsided, the community flourished, financially, intellectually, and spiritually.

This was the pattern until the Inquisition, the expulsion of 1492, when all those who (publicly) refused to convert were exiled, most to Portugal (from where they were exiled again several years later), North Africa, and Turkey, among other places. From this point onward, the Anusim became far greater in numbers. Those who remained in Spain, or near Spain, and were identified as Anusim, became almost an isolated group. Many descendants of Anusim lived in the large Catalonian region, including some in the adjacent island of Majorca. A current resident of Shiloh, Rabbi Nissan Ben-Avraham, originally from Majorca, grew up in a family that was at least partially descended from Anusim. He discovered his Judaism as a teenager, eventually undergoing an extensive learning process to rediscover the heritage that had almost been lost. He is now one of the great Bible teachers in Shiloh, and is the father of twelve children. According to Ben-Avraham, for several centuries after the expulsion of 1492, the Anusim in Majorca could only marry among themselves. "The Gentiles didn't want us and the Jews (usually regular tourists to the island) didn't want us. The Gentiles persecuted us as Jews, even though we went to church and never spoke about Judaism." In fact, there was an absolute unwritten taboo against speaking about Judaism, one that became so ingrained among the Anusim that even after their encounter with freedom of religion in the Western world, it was difficult to overcome the fear. A true story was told of a few descendants of Anusim from Majorca who came to Israel for a visit in 1976. They were speaking to each other and to Israelis, but when one of them started to talk about Judaism, he instinctively switched to a whisper, so no one would hear. As strange and amusing as it seemed to be whispering about Judaism in Israel, the centuries of persecution had taken their toll.

A fascinating phenomenon in our times is that despite the years of separation from their people, and being raised with non-Jewish, usually Catholic religious observance, many thousands of the descendants of Anusim still identify, either secretly or openly, with their Jewish heritage. Grace Fenn, who often calls herself Dona Gracia Fenn, was born in southern Texas to immigrant parents from Spain and Mexico. She describes her personal "awakening":

> *"...we were always recognized as 'different'. I discovered this secret (of her Jewish roots) upon my first trip to Israel, when I recognized many Israelis as similar to myself. After about a year of research, I confronted my father, then 87 years of age and he told me the truth plainly – 'Somos Judios' (We are Jews)."*

"So many of these Jews were lost through the centuries of persecution, forced conversions, and eventually, intermarriage, but the spark of Israel remained alive in so many others, despite the severe and ongoing persecution, or maybe because of it."

Margalit Serra, another Shiloh resident, and a former resident of Catalonia referred to that incredibly resilient Jewish spark when she pointed out that, "Almost all of the Catalonian people were considered as Jews by the Spaniards. This was due to our many Jewish values and our unusual and persistent interest in Israel, but we weren't even Jews!"

"Israel amidst the nations is like the heart amidst the organs of the body; it is at one and the same time the most sick and the healthiest of them." (Yehudah Halevi, The Kuzari 2:36)

Through the centuries of exile, the Jewish people provided spiritual sustenance to the world, or at least to those who were open to receiving it. As discussed earlier, great works of spirituality and moral wisdom were produced, while simultaneously, or intermittently, the oppression and persecution were overwhelming. Despite some wonderful periods of wealth, religious renewal, and creativity, the "wandering Jew" had no rest and stability in the exile. Thus, the concept of the wandering Jew, forever running from place to place. But this was all part of the Divine plan.

The Jewish communities of Spain were eventually, to a great extent, re-established in the countries of the Muslim world, such as Turkey, Morocco, Egypt, and Syria, while much smaller numbers made it to the Land of Israel (then commonly known as Palestine).

"I scattered them among the nations and they were dispersed among the lands; according to their way and according to their acts did I judge them." (Ezekiel 36:19)

"You only have I known of all the families of the earth, and therefore, I will hold you to account for all of your iniquities." (Amos 3:2)

Russia and Eastern Europe

Some of the most significant movements, as well as some of the most vicious forms of Anti-Semitism (Anti-Jewish hatred) originated in the Russian Empire and other parts of Eastern Europe. The impact of these movements resonates in Israel and the world to this day.

The spread of the Russian Empire in the 18th century had certain unintended effects, specifically the increase in its Jewish population. As a result of the annexation of a substantial portion of Poland in 1772, Russia inherited 200,000 Jews. Through the subsequent partitions of 1793 and 1795, which added other Polish-Lithuanian provinces to the empire, the number of Jews grew to 900,000. These annexations and/or partitions presented the Russians with a dilemma. Their historic prejudices prevented them from allowing the Jews to integrate with the Russian population, so specific ordinances were enacted, limiting Jewish residence, work, and movement to certain provinces and districts. This came to be known as the Pale of Settlement. (Louis Greenberg, The Jews In Russia, 1976)

"And it is a looted, downtrodden people, all of them trapped in holes, and hidden away in prisons; they are looted and there is no res-

cuer; plundered with none to say, 'Give it back!' Who among you will give ear to this, will hearken and hear the outcome?" (Isaiah 42:22-23)

Even those Jews living outside of the Pale of Settlement had restrictions placed on their work options, effectively making it almost impossible for them to work in most parts of the Russian Empire. These measures became more and more intense in the 19th century, and the late 1800s saw pogroms (organized massacres) throughout the Russian Empire. These organized physical attacks on Jews, in which their property and businesses were plundered and many individual Jews beaten or worse, with the acquiescence of the Russian authorities, became more and more brutal, culminating in the mass expulsion of the Jews from Moscow in 1891-1892.
(Encyclopaedia Judaica, Vol.13, Pp.696-697)

Out of this background of ongoing oppression, emerged three significant Jewish movements:

♦ Socialism
♦ The Haskalah (Enlightenment Movement)
♦ Zionism

Socialism, while not just a Jewish movement, was one that many Jews were involved in. This clearly stemmed from their idealism, from the Jewish desire to create a better world. Consequently, many of the early leaders of the Bolshevik Revolution were Jews, but their influence waned as Communism took hold in the Soviet Union. Nonetheless, the Socialist/Communist influence was strong in the early years of the State of Israel, and some of its aspects, both negative and positive remain to this day..

The Haskalah was a movement to acquire an extensive secular (university) education, unfortunately, often at the expense of the extensive religious education that Jews had been receiving up to that time. Socialism aimed to create a utopian (ideal) society based, at least in theory, on economic equality and cooperation, while Zionism was the political movement to create a Jewish state, preferably in the Land of Israel. Zionism was influenced by both of the other movements. While some of the earliest settlers in the latter part of the 19th century were religious Zionists, most of the early Zionists tended to be secular, well-versed in secular education, and often dogmatic believers in the Socialist system. The Zionist movement sent a steady stream of Jews to the Land of Israel in the late 19th century and the early part of the 20th century. They worked under very difficult conditions, many of them draining the swamps and developing the agriculture in the early settlements, some of which eventually became cities. Many Jews died of malaria and other diseases and suffered from severe poverty, but the goal of settling the Land was paramount, and great sacrifice was expected. This idealism captured the hearts and yearnings of Jewish people around the world, as well as everyone who could appreciate the Biblical significance of the return of Israel to its ancestral homeland. The excitement of seeing the desert bloom and the Land once again giving of its fruit was a miraculous happening.

"People will say, 'This very land, which had been desolate, has become like the Garden of Eden; and the ruined, desolate, and demolished cities have been fortified, inhabited!' The nations that remain around you will know that I, the Lord, have rebuilt the ruins and I have replanted the wasteland; I, the Lord, have spoken and I shall act." (Ezekiel 36:35-36)

In 1917, the Balfour Declaration was proclaimed by England, and subsequently endorsed by the League of Nations, authorizing the British rulers of the Land of Israel to work towards the creation of a Jewish homeland in the land that they were calling Palestine. It should be noted that the territory consisted of all of present-day Israel, including Judea, Samaria, and Gaza, plus all of the territory of present-day Jordan, east of the Jordan River, which had been the inheritance of the Israelite tribes of Gad, Reuven, and half of the tribe of Manasseh, but was given by the British to the Hashemite family from western Arabia in 1923 to create a new Arab state in 76.8% of British Mandatory "Palestine."

The flow of Jewish immigration became, by necessity, partially covert in the late 1930s into the 1940s, when the British rulers, under Arab pressure, drastically limited the amount of Jewish refugees allowed in. The Arabs fought the (up to that point) growing Jewish immigration every way they could, including massive pogroms in the cities of Safed, Hebron, and Jerusalem. These brutal attacks, in 1920, 1921, 1929, 1936-39, and throughout the 1940s, victimized hundreds of peaceful Jewish civilians who were murdered, raped, robbed, and left homeless and orphaned. The Arab population of the Land of Israel did everything in its power to prevent the massive influx of Jewish refugees that would eventually come as a result of WWII and the Holocaust in Germany and the rest of Europe. An Arab-Nazi alliance (see Encyclopaedia Judaica, Volume 8) was formed as Haj Amin al-Husseini, the leader of the Arabs in the Land of Israel at that time, was welcomed in Berlin as Nazi leader Adolf Hitler's personal guest. He did everything in his power to stop the rescue of Jewish refugees from the death camps, reportedly even visiting Auschwitz and planning the construction of a replica in Shechem, in the Samarian region of Israel, a sinister plan that obviously never came to fruition.

Not that the rest of the free world was much more helpful in welcoming in the Jewish refugees fleeing Europe and their eventual annihilation. Even the United States, which had been very welcoming to Jewish immigrants in the early part of the century, now refused to bend its restrictive immigration quotas as late as 1939, to take in large numbers of refugees fleeing the persecution and almost certain death. The Nazis mocked the hypocrisy of the free world:

> "We are saying openly that we do not want the Jews, while the democracies keep on claiming that they are willing to receive them – and then leave the guests out in the cold! Aren't we savages better men after all?"
>
> *(Der Weltkampf, August 1939)*

Most of the world leaders turned their eyes away from the Nazi persecution of the Jews, and even Hitler's invasion of much of Europe, until they couldn't ignore it any longer and the Allies, the United States, the Soviet Union, and England, went to war against the Nazi armies, but the fate of the Jews, being herded like cattle to the death camps was not a top priority.

> "Their fate has no place on the agendas of the Big Three. Nor does it rouse the conscience of nations. Writers, artists, moralists: some are absorbed by their work, their immortality, others by the conflict in its totality. Everything proceeds as though the Jews did not exist, as though they existed no more. As though Auschwitz (the notorious death camp) were but a

peaceful town somewhere in Silesia. President Roosevelt refuses to bomb the railroad tracks leading to it. When con-
sulted, Winston Churchill concurs in the refusal. Moscow con-
demns German atrocities perpetrated against civilian populations, but blankets in silence the massacre of the Jews. On
both sides, they are sacrificed in advance. People will say: History
will judge. Indeed. But it will judge without understanding."
(Elie Wiesel, One Generation After, P.51)

Six years later, in 1945, the war came to an end and the Allies
were victorious. But for the Jews of Europe, it was already too late.
Six million Jews, including one million children, had been murdered
in the Nazi gas chambers and crematoria, and most of the survivors
were scarred for life.

"Look from heaven and perceive that we have become an object of
scorn and derision among the nations; we are regarded as the sheep led
to slaughter, to be killed, destroyed, beaten and humiliated. But despite
all this, we have not forgotten Your Name – we beg You not to forget us."
(Tachanun prayer)

Despite the efforts of the Arab Muslim leader Husseini and his
ilk, who had worked hand in hand with the Nazi leadership, many of
the survivors made it to the Land of Israel, to the only land that had
ever been divinely promised to any people. Then in 1947, the famous
United Nations resolution was passed, approving the partition of Palestine into Jewish and Arab states, in effect approving the establishment of the State of Israel. Despite their misgivings, it had to be
acceptable to the Zionist leadership that the U.N. was only legitimiz-
ing less than 20% of the Balfour-mandated territory as the State of
Israel. They weren't willing to renounce Israel's claim to the entire
Land of Israel, but they saw this as a necessary first step, and were
prepared to work within the reality and danger of a temporarily truncated state.

On May 15, 1948, the State of Israel was declared, and the Arab
forces, surrounding Israel on all sides and within Israel itself, immediately launched coordinated attacks to destroy the nascent state. This
was the Israeli War of Independence. Thank God, the attempts to
prevent the rise of the state failed, but the results of the war were

extremely painful, both in terms of deaths and territory lost. A full one percent of the Jewish population of the newborn state had been killed in the fighting, half of whom were civilians. The historic, Biblical regions of Judea and Samaria and eastern Jerusalem were captured by Jordan, the state that had been created by the British some twenty-five years prior, on the eastern side of the Jordan River, to placate the Hashemite family in Saudi Arabia, by putting one of its native sons on the throne. Gaza was taken by Egypt and the Syrians occupied the Golan Heights.

Israel was left with a tiny state, a thin strip of coastal land in the west-central part of the country where most of its cities and population were, a dangerous situation that former Israeli Foreign Minister Abba Eban called Israel's "Auschwitz Borders" of 1948-1967, referring cynically to the notorious Holocaust-era concentration camp where so many Jews were brutally murdered. The security risk was real and palpable, but the existential risk of our claim to the Land was that much greater.

As a result of the war, Israel was left without its raison d'etre, its Biblical heartland. This wasn't just a security concern, but a much deeper problem. The richness of Israel's history was imbedded in the mountains of Samaria, in the Judean hills, and in the eastern neighborhoods of Jerusalem. The first Israelites, Abraham and Sarah didn't stroll on the promenade of Tel Aviv, Joshua didn't speak to the people in the shopping malls of Netanya, and Samuel the Prophet didn't issue his warnings from the beaches of Herzliya, for all of these cities were established in the past 100 years of political Zionism. But Abraham was tested by God on Mount Moriah (the Temple Mount) in (eastern) Jerusalem, Joshua the Ephraimite did preach to His People in Shiloh, which is in Samaria, and the Patriarchs and Matriarchs of Israel are buried in the Judean city of Hebron.

While the thin nine-mile coastal strip of 1948-1967 Israel was a very urgent security concern, the greatest existential threat to Israel was the loss of its historical places, which were the most concrete evidence of its deep roots in the Land of Israel. The Arab armies sensed this vulnerability and pounced on it, massing their troops along Israel's borders, causing the Six-Day-War of 1967. Israel was vastly outnumbered by the Arab nations, both in manpower and in weaponry, but its leaders showed that they understood the advantages of psychological warfare, by preempting the expected attacks and taking the offensive. Some highlights from the war:

"On the morning of June 5th, the Israeli air force attacked the airfields of Egypt, Jordan, Iraq, and Syria, destroying 452 planes – 391 of them on the ground – in under three hours and achieving complete superiority in the air...

"By dawn on Friday June 9th, Israel forces were encamped along the (Suez) Canal and the Gulf of Suez. The Egyptians had had over 400 tanks destroyed and 200 captured, losing more than 10,000 men and 12,000 prisoners...

"By June 7th, Israel was in control of Nablus (Shechem), Ramallah, Jericho, and Bethlehem. It was now possible to start the historic battle for the Old City (of Jerusalem), which was taken by a paratroop unit breaking in through St. Stephen's (Lions') Gate in hand-to-hand fighting to avoid any damage to the holy places. By the evening, the whole of Samaria and Judea were in Israel's hands."

(Encyclopaedia Judaica, Volume 9, Pp.410-411)

Yes, the battles were fierce, but when the war was finished just six days later, Israel had won a massive victory, recapturing all of the historic lands that it had lost in the War of Independence. It recaptured the holy sites – Shiloh, Hebron, Beth El, Bethlehem, Shechem, the Temple Mount, and the Old City of Jerusalem – all fell into Israel's hands, swiftly and triumphantly. All of these holy sites had not been under sovereign Jewish control for almost 2,000 years! What a Kiddush Hashem (sanctification of God's Name) we were witnessing! The world watched with eyes wide open as the descendants of King David won the war in six days, and on the seventh day they rested, because the war had ended and because it was the Sabbath. Such an opportunity stood before Israel at that moment. How would they react to this great, miraculous victory? What nation wins a war in six days and on the seventh day they rest, winning back their Biblical heartland, the cradle of their civilization? Surely, they would sing God's praises in thanksgiving for the good that He had done for them! After the Six-Day-War, it no longer mattered that much of secular Israel had previously claimed not to believe in God. How could anyone witness such miraculous events and remain an atheist?

"This people I have formed for Myself, that they might declare My praise." (Isaiah 43:21)

Alas, with the exception of much of the religious sector of Israel's population, which saw the events as nothing less than miraculous, and a significant stage in the redemptive process, most Israelis saved their praise for mortal man. What a great army we have, went the refrain. The myth of the Israeli soldier-hero was proclaimed around the world at that time, and to a lesser extent, continues to be worshipped, almost as a false idol to this day.

Yes, we do have a good army, but as we discussed earlier, its strength is derived from its Maker, and our ability to succeed in war is directly dependent on our Father in Heaven. Joshua Bin Nun and King David were great warriors, but they were guided by the will of God, and they often expressed their eagerness to follow in His path. When they succeeded in war, they made it abundantly clear that they knew Who was responsible.

"There is no wisdom nor understanding nor counsel against the Lord; the horse is prepared for the day of battle, but victory is from the Lord." (Proverbs 21:30-31)

When we truly believe that, there is no limit to how high we can go. Our challenge in Israel is to see God's presence in all of our actions and in all events that occur in the world, but too many of our people in Israel and elsewhere have taken on a very different world view. This is a world view that is based on atheism and places man at the center, as opposed to the King of the Universe. This is a philosophy of life that is contrary to the Bible, which places the covenant between the God of Israel and His People on center stage. When we ignore this basic fact, we imperil not only ourselves, but the entire world, because the spiritual ramifications of our actions reverberate around the world.

Chapter Six

Returning To The Heartland

"I shall yet rebuild you and you shall be rebuilt, O Maiden of Israel; you will yet adorn yourself with drums and go forth in the dance of merrymakers. You will yet plant vineyards in the mountains of Samaria; the planters will plant and redeem."
(Jeremiah 31:3-4)

The miraculous victory in the Six-Day-War of 1967 carried out by the vastly outnumbered and surrounded Israel military brought varying reactions from people around the world, but hardly anybody was neutral. For Jews around the world, it was a source of enormous pride, enabling them to hold their heads higher. After almost 2,000 years of being the vulnerable, persecuted Jew of the exile, here was a chance for the Russian, American, British, French, and other Jews to be proud of their Israeli brethren, who had boldly liberated the lands of their heritage. For the Arabs, especially the Muslim Arabs, it was a bitter defeat for the Koranic vision of the subservient Jew. The Arabs of Hebron and other cities where terrible pogroms against innocent Jewish civilians had been carried out in the 1920s and 1930s, cowered in fear, fully expecting the victors to now seek revenge for the crimes that had been committed against their brethren.

"And the peoples heard and were in great fear; trembling gripped the dwellers of Philistia." (Exodus 15:14)

The Arab fears proved to be unfounded, as no such revenge action was undertaken, whether justifiable or not. Perhaps it was because of the Israeli leaders' hypersensitivity to world opinion, or perhaps it was never even considered because Jews just don't view revenge in the same way Arabs do. Another possibility is that Israel was so absorbed in the euphoria of the great victory to even think of such an act of vengeance once the war had ended. After all, the Israeli military had just defeated multiple Arab armies that were far more numerous and better armed than the Israeli forces. This was indeed a cause for great celebration!

"You will pursue your enemies and they will fall before you by the sword. Five of you will pursue a hundred, and a hundred of you will pursue ten thousand..." (Leviticus: 7-8)

But the great reaction, both positive and negative, that this victory caused among Jews and Arabs, was only the tip of the iceberg. The United Nations condemned Israel for defending itself and winning. On the other hand, many Biblically-literate people from around the world were ecstatic, as the victory was rightly viewed as at least a partial fulfillment of the prophetic vision of the return of Israel to its Biblical heartland.

"I will sanctify my great Name that was desecrated among the nations, which you have desecrated among them; then the nations will know that I am the Lord... when I become sanctified through you before their eyes. I will take you from among the nations, and gather you out of all countries and will bring you to your own soil." (Ezekiel 36:23-24)

The Six Day War was a miraculous occurrence through which the world could gradually see the prophecies coming alive in the Promised Land. Those who were familiar with what those prophecies said about Israel's return were understandably excited about the miraculous liberation of the ancient holy sites. It was properly viewed by many of them as the clear evidence of God's existence and active role in this world, acting through His People. The ingathering of the exiles that had mushroomed after 1948, with the arrival of hundreds of thousands of Jews from the Arab countries of the Middle East and the Holocaust survivors, was given a boost of "positive Aliyah", immigration to Israel, as thousands of Jews from the free world, even from the U.S.A., wanted to take part in this exciting enterprise that had captured the world's imagination.

Unfortunately, the excitement didn't captivate everybody and didn't last forever, and once the euphoria of the Six-Day-War had worn off, questions began to be raised about what to do with the liberated territories that had fallen into Israel's hands. Rather than immediately declaring those areas an integral part of Israel and establishing new communities in all the ancient cities that we read about in the Bible, the prevailing position in the political establishment, to varying degrees, called for using the territories of Judea, Samaria, and Gaza as political bargaining chips to be given to the Arabs in exchange for a peace agreement. In their eyes, the Land had no intrinsic value, but was just a tool through which a peace agreement could be negotiated.

The loss of will became manifest almost immediately after the war. Shortly after the fighting had ended, the Israeli government leaders rushed to Hebron to assure the Muslim authorities that the Cave of the Patriarchs and Matriarchs, where Abraham, Isaac, and Jacob, Sarah, Rebecca, and Leah are buried, would remain in Muslim hands. In Jerusalem, the former capital of the unified Kingdom of Israel, they went one step further, with then Defense Minister Moshe Dayan ordering the heads of the Israeli Defense Forces to remove the Israeli flag from the Temple Mount and returning the Temple Mount key to the Muslim Wakf religious authorities. The Temple Mount had been returned to Israel through the grace of God, and the blind politicians failed to see what was in front of their eyes. Thus, in one fell swoop, they handed over the authority for the site where Solomon's Temple had once stood in all of its glory until it was destroyed by Nebuchadnezzar, where the Second Temple had stood until destroyed by the Romans, and where many centuries earlier, when that hill was known simply as Mount Moriah, the Almighty had put Abraham and his son Isaac to the ultimate test.

"Do not stretch out your hand against the lad nor do anything to him for now I know that you are a God fearing man, since you have not withheld your son, your only son, from me." (Genesis 22:12)

To the modern mind, the story of Abraham and Isaac seems bizarre. God tells him to kill his son and Abraham calmly goes about the task? What father in our times can seriously relate to such a situation? The faith of Abraham and his absolute trust that God would never instruct him in the wrong way stands out among the great Biblical stories of faith. The message is clear: When we need to choose

between God's instructions and our own "common sense," we need to follow His lead in even the most extreme circumstances. Yet, in 1967, after the most miraculous of victories, after winning the war in only six days, an event that should have put an end to Israeli atheism, the political leadership of Israel, fearing what the world would say, fearing mortal man more than the King of kings, failed its own test of faith. By not waving the Israeli flag over the Temple Mount and proclaiming, with Bible in hand, "This is my God, and this is His Land and He has returned it to His People!" the Israeli leaders proved that they weren't yet ready to receive this gift from God. Sadly, the Israeli government didn't choose to, or lacked the necessary under-standing, to provide the leadership of faith needed to respond to the Lord's challenge. As we discussed earlier, what nation wins a war in six days and on the seventh day they rest? Is this a people whose destiny is governed simply by pragmatism? Does the return of the Biblical heartland to God's Chosen People in just six days not imply a spiritual challenge to be met?

"...but you, O mountains of Israel, will give forth your branch and bear your fruit for My people Israel, for they are soon to come...I will make people numerous upon you – the entire House of Israel, all of it; the cities will be inhabited and the ruins will be rebuilt." (Ezekiel 36:8,10)

That spiritual challenge was met by many of the Israeli people at the grassroots level, who went out to reclaim what had been taken away from them. On the eve of the Passover holiday in 1968, several men and women and their many children stayed at the Park Hotel in the middle of Arab-occupied Hebron and celebrated the holiday of freedom there. They declared their intention to stay in Hebron, claim-ing that they had returned home thirty-nine years after the pogrom of 1929. A long period of national debate ensued, and after difficult negotiations with the government, temporary compromises were reached that eventually led to the renewal of limited Jewish settle-ment in the city of Hebron. Other parts of Judea followed, but per-mission to renew settlement in the Biblical heartland of Samaria, lo-cated north of Jerusalem, were not as forthcoming. It wasn't until after the Yom Kippur War in 1973 that things started to move.

The Yom Kippur War had caught Israel off-guard and it was very painful, with many Israeli soldiers killed and wounded. In contrast to the Six-Day-War, the mood of the country was somber, and the need for a renewal of the Zionist vision was great. That sense of idealism and initiative was provided by the great Rabbi Tzvi Yehuda Kook, an old sage with a long white beard who personally led many of his students who went out to settle the Samarian hills. The pattern that had been started in Hebron and other parts of Judea (south of Jerusalem) was continued in Samaria (north of Jerusalem), as the Seed of Shiloh was formed, a group of very young, idealistic Jews, intending to settle the ancient capital in the center of the Biblical heartland, up in the hills of Ephraim. However, permission to do so was not readily forthcoming from the government, which as usual was concerned about American and European opposition, so the attention of the group was temporarily redirected to other parts of Samaria. It was clear to them that settling other parts of Samaria would eventually make it possible to reach their goal, of re-establishing the ancient city where Joshua had long ago urged the tribes of Israel to claim their inheritance throughout the Land.

"How long will you wait, to come and take possession of the land that the Lord, God of your fathers has given you?" (Joshua 18:3)

"...and they will inherit the fields of Ephraim and Samaria..." (Obadiah 1:19)

The southernmost area of the portion of Ephraim was the first to receive government approval for settlement, when the community of Ofra was unofficially set up in April of 1975, ostensibly as an important military installation. Being situated on one of the highest elevations in central Israel, Ofra was certainly militarily strategic, but the intention was to settle the Land and build a community. Ofra became the organizational base for the Seed of Shiloh, and from there other young people were invited to join the challenge. At that time, Ofra was a good thirty minute roundabout ride to Shiloh and since most of these 21 to 25-year-olds didn't have cars, it made the task all the more difficult when the moment arrived to make the big move.

On the first day of the Hebrew month of Shvat (January 9, 1978), the first Jews returned as residents of the reborn ancient capital. An official permit was soon given, confirming the return to Shiloh as an "archeological expedition." That was the official spin, not one that was taken too seriously by anybody, neither its supporters nor its opponents, notwithstanding the archeological significance of the site. Just two weeks later, a great ceremony was held on the then barren, rocky hills of Shiloh, which had been waiting for its children to return home for close to two thousand years. Rabbi Tzvi Yehuda Kook, then eighty-four years old and not in the greatest physical health made the difficult, winding one hour drive to be there, along with other rabbis and activists and the brave pioneers who were finally succeeding in re-establishing roots in the place where the permanent Tabernacle had stood for 369 years.

Despite the official designation, it was announced at this ceremony that the foundation stone was being laid for the building of a "new" city in Israel. It created quite a commotion in Israel and the world, as the enemies of Israel, as well as their Israeli apologists, recognized the significance of the return to Shiloh. One of the founders of the return to Shiloh recalled the far-left Israeli politician, Yossi Sarid, feigning a lack of concern, by saying that after a few months the settlers would leave, as a result of the difficult living conditions. It's true, indeed, that the physical living conditions left a lot to be desired. Electricity was provided only by a noisy generator, while water was carried in from a natural well, located down in the adjacent valley. There was one primitive and not so reliable military telephone, used by the soldiers on duty, as well as by the eight families and the twenty singles who were the first residents of Shiloh. The singles lived in tents at first, while the young families lived in 22 square meter caravans (no-frills trailer homes). The living conditions weren't easy, but it was a privilege to be among the first returnees to the ancient capital, so such inconveniences were easily ignored.

As we discussed earlier, the city of Shiloh in the days of Joshua, Hannah, and Samuel the Prophet may have been the capital and home of the Tabernacle for 369 years, but it also represented the adolescent stage of Israel's history. An interesting parallel can be drawn between the theme of adolescence and the struggle for maturity and independence as represented by the Seed of Shiloh. The very young adults who came to Shiloh to re-establish the ancient capital had a clear sense of purpose and single-minded devotion to their cause. It didn't matter that most of them were barely twenty-three years old. It didn't matter that several of the women were pregnant and living quite far from the nearest hospital, with no means of transportation during

The Seed of Shiloh Returns Home: *The original prefabricated homes and structures of the re-established Shiloh community – February 1978.*

daytime hours, while their husbands were at work. Shiloh was very isolated, and the nearest ambulance was many miles away. As one of the founders, Meir Stein, explains it, "Yes, several of the women were pregnant during those first few months. In fact, my wife was pregnant with twins, but nobody was too concerned. We were optimists and we felt that everything would work out for the best. Our parents and everyone else thought we were crazy to give up our comfortable lives in the cities to settle the heartland, but the truth is, we didn't care what anyone thought about us – the world, our parents, the government, or the media." Yes, they had the idealism, and perhaps the almost care-free determination that adolescents or young adults often have. But there the psychological parallels end, for there was no confused search for identity. They knew who they were, why they were there, and Who gave them the right to be there.

"Every place upon which the sole of your foot shall tread, I have given to you, as I spoke to Moses. From the desert and this Lebanon until the great river, the Euphrates River, all the land of the Hittites until the Great Sea toward the setting of the sun shall be your border." (Joshua 1:3-4)

The first eight families enjoyed their first year together. They enjoyed the excitement of building a new community, all the more so since it happened to be in the first ancient capital of Israel, and they were determined to make it work. Whatever social or logistic obstacles got in their way, solutions would be found, for they were making history here, and nothing could get in the way of that.

In modern Israel, young couples would often take a break from their newfound independence to visit their parents for the holidays, but on the first Passover in Shiloh, all of the young couples, as well as the singles, decided to spend Passover together in Shiloh. The social harmony among these young, mostly native-born Israelis was remarkable, but it was almost like living in a carefully controlled test tube. As the community grew, it took the risk of losing that carefully constructed, blissful state of affairs, but grow it did. The goal was never to remain a small community of only twenty families, but to rebuild the ancient city.

Within ten to fifteen years, the central community of Shiloh expanded to encompass families of many different ethnic groups and countries of origin. Some neighborhoods in Shiloh became an amazing mix of cultures. In the present population of Shiloh, there are now families tracing not-so-distant roots back to Peru, Mexico, Holland, the former Soviet Union, the United States, Canada, New Zealand, England, Burma, Morocco, Lebanon, Syria, Yemen, Thailand, Ethiopia, Argentina, France, Iran, Majorca, Catalonia, and of course native-born Israelis of many generations in Israel. Despite their diverse backgrounds and countries of origin, these immigrants are all integrally bound to the Land. One elderly immigrant from Russia, a former officer in the Soviet army named Zechariah Begun, used to volunteer his impressive gardening skills for different families in Shiloh, and would never take money for his services. When once offered payment, the then energetic eighty-year-old responded," How can I take money for planting in the Land of Israel? I see it as my duty!" The immigrants had returned home to their heartland in Shiloh inspired by a fierce idealism that often opens the eyes of many visitors and reminds them that Zionism is alive and well in the heartland communities. Hebrew may be a second language for many of these immigrants, and they may all come from very different cultures and mentalities, but they are bound together by their love of the Land and their belief in God and His Torah.

"I will take you from among the nations and gather you from all the

lands, and I will bring you to your own soil." (Ezekiel 36:24)

"Behold, I will bring them from the land of the North, and gather them from the ends of the earth. Among them will be the blind and the lame, the pregnant and the birthing together; a great congregation will return here. With weeping they will come and through supplications I will bring them; I will guide them on streams of water, on a direct path in which they will not stumble; for I have been a father to Israel, and Ephraim is my firstborn." (Jeremiah 31:7-8)

The prophetic nature of this ingathering in the hills of Ephraim was awe-inspiring, but it was often overshadowed by the day-to-day difficulties of life. The growth and absorption process in Shiloh wasn't always easy, and there were occasionally conflicts and disputes between different people, different groups of people, or different sectors in the community. This was painful for those who remembered, or knew of, the extraordinary social cohesion of the original group, but it was a necessary stage of growth. Just as the Children of Israel's years in Ancient Shiloh were a necessary "adolescent" period of difficult growth, learning, and exploration with a newfound autonomy, so too, the young community of the re-established Shiloh needed to go through its own "adolescent" period of occasional internal dissension, combined with slow, but steady growth. As Meir Stein explained, "No one says that mistakes weren't made along the way. We were lacking in experience and maturity, but we knew that it was important for the community, and for the goal of settling the Land, to bring in different kinds of people and to learn to live together." The growing community of Shiloh in a sense became a microcosm for the country as a whole, with veteran Israelis and immigrants from all over the world learning to live together and gradually to appreciate the important roles that each could play in the building up of Shiloh.

Not only the central community, but many of the adjacent hilltops were settled as well. One of these newer communities, established in 1984, was named Eli, after the high priest in Shiloh, and was formed with the original goal of being a large community of secular and religious living together. It rapidly expanded to encompass quite a few hilltops. Another community, established in the same year, was called Maale Levonah, named after the ancient city Levonah.

"Behold, there is a yearly holiday unto the Lord at Shiloh, which is north of Beth El, east of the road going up from Beth El to Shechem, and south of Levonah." (Judges 21:19)

Rachel Druk

In 1991, there was a terror attack on a bus traveling to Tel Aviv. Among the many Shiloh residents on that bus was a woman named Rachel Druk, the mother of seven children. She was shot dead by the terrorists' gunfire, thus becoming the first of many terror victims from Shiloh. After the murder, there were demonstrations demanding that the government establish a new community at the site of the murder, which was about ten minutes north of Shiloh. Those demands were not met right away, but a more immediate compromise was reached, in which the government agreed to establish a new neighborhood adjacent to the existing Shiloh community, which would be called Shvut Rachel, or Rachel's Return. That neighborhood, established in 1991, has grown to be a thriving community in its own right.

In the succeeding years, many of our other once barren hilltops have been settled, usually by young, idealistic couples and young families, attracted by the excitement and optimism that guided the original settlers of Shiloh in 1978. Before long, each rocky hilltop was no longer barren, as seeds were sown and trees were planted.

"In the wilderness I will set cedar, acacia, myrtle and pine tree..." (Isaiah 41:19)

Each of these hilltop communities has been given its own name, and developed its own character, ranging from farming and agricultural, to religious hippie or yuppie-suburban, but all are part of what has come to be known as Gush Shiloh, or the Shiloh bloc of communities, a contiguous group of independent but connected communities, with ancient Shiloh at its center. The people of Shiloh work in many different fields and in many different parts of the country. There are numerous "baalei tshuva", or recent returnees to religious life and faith, who enliven the community with their spiritual enthusiasm, love of life, and multi-faceted backgrounds. Shiloh has also been blessed with many artists and craftspeople of all kinds, as well as several accomplished musicians, including Yehuda Glantz, a well-known performer of Latino-Hasidic music.

As one enters the central section of the Shiloh community, called Eli the Cohen (Eli the High Priest), several things stand out that show how much progress has been made in just 28 years. There is a small supermarket in which one can buy Skippy Peanut Butter, Kellogg's Cornflakes, and Pillsbury Cake Mix, in addition to all of the usual Israeli produce. To the right of the supermarket is the community's educational complex which consists of schools, kindergartens, nurseries, and the child development center. In Shiloh, it's not a cliche to say that the children are the future. As of the year 2006, there were over 1,000 families living in Gush Shiloh, with many, many children. In fact, the children dominate the life of the community. Unlike in many suburban communities in the United States and Europe, or even in many places in Israel, the children of Shiloh are ever-present and numerous, riding freely on their bicycles, walking to a late afternoon lesson or activity, or climbing on the same ancient rocks and hills that that were probably trod on by Samuel the Prophet as a young boy in Shiloh. These children are being raised with optimism, strong family values, faith in God and a firm belief in our God-given right to this Land.

Tel Shiloh

Any person possessing a basic knowledge of the psychological and cognitive makeup of children knows that while learning from a book can be very effective, there is nothing like bringing the story to life in a way that is both inspiring and easily understood. The Bible has been described as the all-time bestseller, but unless the stories are told in a very concrete way that helps children to relate to the characters and stories, they remain abstract, and therefore, difficult to relate to. The challenge is to take stories about people who lived several thousand years ago in abstract places called Israel, or Canaan, or Egypt and make it relevant to the young self-centered mind. For all of these reasons, only the best educators, artists, or entertainers can truly bring the great Biblical stories to life for children. When they do, it is a wonderful sight to see. Those who have been fortunate enough to tour the Land of Israel with Bible in hand will tell you that the stories

From the Place Where God's Presence Dwelled*: A woman prays in the tranquility of the Tabernacle site in Shiloh.*

literally come to life before their eyes. In the ancient site of Shiloh, known as Tel Shiloh, one is surrounded by history at every turn. To walk on the very spot where Joshua spoke to the leaders of the tribes, and to read about it in the Book of Joshua; to read the prophetic Hannah's Prayer on the very spot where she prayed for a son and praised the Creator; to read about that son Samuel the Prophet's self-lessness as we walk on the site where his mother selflessly gave him as a gift to God's service; these are all prime examples of the Bible coming to life in our times.

"Samuel took nothing from the community. He did not even drink from the public reservoir." (Midrash HaGadol, Numbers 16:15)

"When the People of Israel saw the cloud suspended between heaven and earth, they knew that God was speaking with Moses. So it was also with Samuel." (Sifri Zuta, Numbers 12:5)

What can be more inspiring for young children than to learn the story of this young boy whose mother's gratitude to God for granting her wish caused her to dedicate him to the Lord's service in Shiloh? Her quiet, but firm and proud prayer resonates to this day in the hills of Shiloh and around the world. The clear lesson is that sincere prayer comes from the heart, and that we are dependent on God for the most basic things in life, but that the Master of the Universe expects us to express what we are feeling and to assert ourselves, even with Him.

The Basilica: *This reconstructed Byzantine Era structure is believed to have been a church, with an impressive mosaic floor.*

Although the founding families of modern Shiloh were certainly drawn to the historical significance of the site, new archeological excavations of the site, which would be the first in over fifty years, didn't begin for several years. Over the previous hundred years, there had been several expeditions to Shiloh. During the years 1871-1878, a team led by Sir Charles Wilson and Sir Charles Warren was sent by Queen Victoria of England to perform a comprehensive geographic and topographic survey of key parts of the Land of Israel west of the Jordan River. This included an in-depth survey of Shiloh. Subsequent archeological excavations by Danish teams in the 1920s and early 1930s discovered ruins from Ancient Shiloh, but there were no other noteworthy digs until Israel's return to Shiloh spurred renewed interest in the first capital of Israel. In 1981, three years after the reestablishment of the Shiloh community, the first serious archeological excavations in decades were carried out at the site of Ancient Shiloh by the Department of Land of Israel Studies of Bar Ilan University, and four seasons of excavation were undertaken.

One opinion that seems to be without dispute from all of these expeditions is that the location of historic Shiloh (known in Arabic as Seilun for several centuries, during the time that the Muslims controlled the Land of Israel) is the same as the present-day Shiloh. On this, the cartographers and archeologists who explored Shiloh seem to concur.

"Shiloh (Judges 21:19) – The undoubted site is the ruin of Seilun." *(The Survey of Western Palestine: Volume Two, Conder and Kitchener, 1882)*

Jamma-Es-Sitten: *The sloped walls (resembling the slightly sloped skins of the Tabernacle in Shiloh) are believed to be ruins of a mosque built during the Muslim Era, on top of the ruins of a Second Temple Era synagogue. There is a convenient space for a Torah scroll on the southern wall, facing Jerusalem, as was already the custom in synagogues at that time. Note the decorative synagogue lintel (center of photo).*

" ...the ancient name of Shiloh was preserved in the name of the Arab village of Seilun, still known in the 16th century, but later deserted. The identification of the site is thus sure. And as we shall see, the excavated remains accord with the history of the site as reflected both in the Bible and in other written sources."

(Biblical Archaeology Review, Jan/Feb.1986)

Although no artifacts from the Tabernacle itself have yet been found, the site of the Tabernacle can be determined, because the dimensions of the only substantial plateau on the Tel clearly fit the Biblical description (see Biblical Archaeology Review, Nov./Dec. 1988). In addition, the structure of the presumed Tabernacle Plateau (according to the above article) would render it quite defendable from enemy attack.

South of the Tabernacle Plateau stand the ruins that the Muslims called Jamma-Es-Sitten, a mosque which archeologists believe was built on the remains of an ancient synagogue, most likely from the Second Temple Era (well over 2,000 years ago). Just north of this site is the site of a reconstructed Byzantine Era church (about 1500 years ago).

Within the structure is an impressive mosaic floor with Greek writing and the star of David, the origins of which are uncertain. Some say that the basic structure was built on the ruins of a synagogue from an earlier period. In another, adjacent location, there is a

Fruit of the Vine: *Mosaic of Grapes at Tel Shiloh*

The Star of David: *Before the Star of David became the symbol of Israel, it was used by both Jews and non-Jews alike. Here it is seen on one of the Mosaic floors at Tel Shiloh.*

relatively small stone structure, believed to have been constructed as a mosque built about 1,000 years ago. It was apparently built on top of the ruins of another Byzantine-era church, dated from approximately the fourth century, as evidenced by the beautiful multi-layered mosaic floors that have been found both under and all around the mosque structure. A baptismal bath, also from the Byzantine-era, was unearthed as well. The excavations at this site, many of which were carried out in 2006, have revealed several Greek inscriptions on the mosaics. Among the various Christian religious inscriptions and probably the name of the artist, there is an inscription on one of the mosaics that asks for divine "mercy for Shiloh and its inhabitants", perhaps referring to the then sorry state of the city that was once the center of Israel's sovereignty and of God's glory. As we've discussed earlier in this chapter, the archeologists and cartographers seem to agree on the location of ancient Shiloh. This early written reference on the mosaic further reinforces and confirms the clear archeological belief that the exact location of historic Shiloh is beyond dispute.

In addition to these finds, the 2006 excavations discovered several substantial walls, often below the level of the mosaics, which

could indicate an earlier period, possibly the Roman
Period or the Second
Temple Period. Clearly,
much more digging will be
needed to clarify these most
recent findings.

In the past few years,
some people have started
referring to the small
mosque structure as the
Synagogue of Hannah's
Prayer, in memory of
Hannah and in recognition
of the many women from
Israel and from all over the
world who, following
Hannah's inspiration, have
come to Tel Shiloh to pray
for children. In Shiloh, we
clearly see the results, as
families of 5-10 children are

*In the Footsteps of Hannah: A group of
Israeli women learning the Biblical sources
in the building known to many as the
Synagogue of Hannah's Prayer.*

not uncommon, but visitors to the site have also been blessed. My
wife and I have received e mails and phone calls from women as far
away as Argentina and New York telling us that their prayers have
been answered. Recently, I was standing outside the Synagogue of
Hannah's Prayer with a group of visitors. After explaining the history of the site, as well as the Biblical story of Hannah, I told the
visitors that they were welcome to go inside and recite some prayers.
There was one very old woman with boundless energy, who the others later told me was about 90 years old, who rushed into the entrance, shouting to everyone, "I'm gonna be like Sarah!" She of course
was alluding to the Biblical Sarah, who miraculously gave birth to
her first child at ninety years of age. No, we haven't received any e
mail or phone announcements from her. Not yet.

*"God had remembered Sarah as He had said; and the Lord did for
Sarah as He had spoken. Sarah conceived and bore a son unto Abraham
in his old age, at the appointed time which God had spoken." (Genesis*

Eli's Apartment? The Cave Entrance seen here was probably used daily by one of the high priests who officiated at the Tabernacle. The cave is believed to have been either a residence or a storage place.

21:1-2)

Archeologists have also discovered burial caves, as well as a cave near the Tabernacle site, which most likely was a dwelling place, perhaps for the High Priest of the Tabernacle. In addition, they have found burnt stones and rocks and carbonized raisins and other foodstuffs, alluding to the great fire and destruction believed to have been carried out by the Philistines when they destroyed Shiloh. These are only some of the fascinating discoveries that have been made in Shiloh during the Bar Ilan University dig and the few earlier excavations, and the few subsequent excavations, but I am convinced that they have only scratched the surface. In an article about Shiloh, which was published back in 1986 in the Biblical Archeology Review, many of the archeological findings up to that point were reported. The title, "Shiloh Yields Some, But Not All, Of Its Secrets", speaks volumes about the need for major funding for extensive excavations in Shiloh, and for its development as a major tourist site. The text of the article alludes to the surprising archeological neglect of this historical region:

"Although this region is located in the heartland of the historical Land of Israel, it is, strangely enough, "terra incognita", archeologically speaking." (Biblical Archeology Review, January/February 1986)

When one sees the huge sums of government money used to develop tourist sites of far less Biblical significance, one has to wonder from where the government of Israel derives its priorities. The archeologist Israel Finkelstein, in a meeting with several local residents in Shiloh at the time of his dig, said that there were more physical remains from the period of Joshua in Shiloh than there were in all of the other archeological sites in Israel combined! Nonetheless, I was also informed that at that very same meeting, when urged to perform a serious dig at the presumed site of the Tabernacle plateau, he rejected the

The Olive Press: *Adjacent to the Tabernacle Plateau is an olive press, which most likely was used as part of the service in the Tabernacle.*

requests, saying that the Tabernacle doesn't interest him. Now I'm

Digging in Shiloh: *Large collar-rim storage jars found during the archeological excavations in Shiloh.*

not an archeologist, and perhaps archeologists have had their own professional reasons for not wanting to focus on the Tabernacle, but it appears to me that the problem is religious/historical. If one believes that Shiloh is our Biblical heartland, then one also believes that we are obligated to do everything in our power to find archeological evidence of the Tabernacle

The Foundation Stone: *This boulder, of a style that dates back to the Second Temple era, was used as one of the foundation stones for the 1,000-year-old mosque structure that is known today by many people as the Synagogue of Hannah's Prayer.*

in order to strengthen our hold on this site, which predated Jerusalem as the capital. Those who view the Bible just as fascinating literature wouldn't feel the same sense of urgency that we do. And that is why this jewel of archeology has been laying relatively dormant for many years. Whatever has been done to develop the tourist site of Tel Shiloh to date, has been accomplished mainly through the great effort and self-sacrifice of those who have worked at the site, with the help of one of the Zionist organizations, from the ongoing taxes of Shiloh residents, and from the steady flow of enthusiastic visitors from around the world.

I hope and pray that we will soon see a shift in government priorities, and that Tel Shiloh will receive the attention that it truly deserves, as the cradle of our civilization in the Land of Israel. For if we truly wish to bolster our claim to the Land of Israel based on the past, we need to climb its rocky hills and explore its wealth of history, in order to create its future. Only these mountains, with their seemingly endless Biblical stories and prophecies, can justify our right to the 100-year-old modern coastal cities, such as Tel Aviv. Only when that fact is understood, will we be able to move forward with a clear belief in the rightness of Israel's path.

Chapter Seven

Plans For Peace

"For they have healed the hurt of the daughter of my people slightly, saying, 'Peace, peace - when there is no peace.'"
(Jeremiah 8:11)

Ah, to have peace. Peace from all of our enemies. While real peace from our enemies' swords has always been desired by all of Israel, the real, usually unasked question has always been, "What is the best way to achieve such peace, and furthermore, is it a realistic goal in our times?" This lusting for peace with our enemies seems to have become an obsession for a large segment of the Israeli (Jewish) population that sees in it a placebo that will bring with it "a normal life." Oh, how wonderful it would be to be a normal people! How nice it would be to live our lives without fear of terrorism. Not to worry about our children serving in the army. To be able to focus on domestic issues like schooling, social security, and childcare. This desire for "normalcy" and acceptance by the world is so pervasive, so strong among most secular Israelis that it can blind the eyes of very intelligent or at least formally-educated people. In such an inferior emotional state, issues fail to be addressed on their merits, and crucial matters of life and death are determined by the question, "Will the world approve?"

It's not easy to be a Jew, as the saying goes, but for much of the secular portion of the People of Israel, the difficulty doesn't refer to the great responsibility that comes with the yoke of heaven, with the commandments. No, for them, it refers to the wars and the terrorism and the feeling of isolation. Most secular Israelis would tell you, "We're exhausted. We're tired of worrying about our children in the army. We're sick of worrying about terrorism. We can't continue living like this as an outcast nation. Sure there's terrorism, but the Arabs say that if we give them a Palestinian state they'll give us peace. We have to give peace a chance because we can't go on like this." Give peace a chance? It was a popular song in the late 1960s, and John Lennon was a talented song writer and maybe even an idealist, but I somehow doubt that he was thinking of the threat from Al Qaeda, Hamas, and Islamic Jihad when he wrote those words. Israelis, Americans or others who try to apply incongruous slogans to the realities of the Middle East are misguided at best, and in effect invite terrorism, causing great suffering with their naivete.

This kind of defeatist thinking among Israelis, blaming the lack of peace on Israel, despite all the evidence to the contrary, has increasingly infected the secular elites that rule the country. Speaking to the Israel Policy Forum in the United States in June of 2005, then Deputy Prime Minister Ehud Olmert epitomized this malaise, saying, "We are tired of fighting, we are tired of being courageous, we are tired of winning, we are tired of defeating our enemies." This man, who was supposedly representing the State of Israel, the country that was established on the ashes of the Holocaust, to insure that Jews would never again go like sheep to the slaughter; this man is tired of winning? Has the State of Israel, created to put an end to that image of weakness, actually traded its post-Holocaust will to survive for a willingness to commit suicide?

Dr. Kenneth Levin, an instructor of clinical psychiatry at Harvard Medical School and a Princeton-trained historian, has referred to the behavior of large segments of the Israeli population as "delusional" and compared such behavior to that of abused children:

> "Abused children always blame themselves for the abuse because they want to believe that they can have control over a situation that is really beyond their control."
> "The hope is that if they just accept the indictment, if they just repress the recognition that they are being attacked unfairly, and try to change accordingly that somehow they'll win relief from their attackers."
> *(Israel National News, March 26, 2006)*

Such delusional thinking has guided Israeli policy makers for several decades. For many years, segments of the Israeli populace have advocated the concept of "land for peace", meaning the tiny State of Israel, smaller in size than New Jersey, would be obligated to give vital portions of its miniscule land in exchange for promises of peace from the Arabs. This has been the basis for the overwhelming majority of Middle East peace plans that have been proposed since the establishment of the State of Israel in 1948. Almost all world leaders seem to accept the basic premise that all Israel needs to do to create peace in the Middle East is to withdraw from "The Occupied Territories," otherwise called "The West Bank." If so, it is presumed, the Arabs will forever live with us in eternal harmony, or at least will accept a truncated state as the best they can get.

In reality, there are no such places as the West Bank or the Occupied Territories. Any child in Israel or elsewhere who has opened a Bible knows that there are no such places, but that there is a region called Samaria, to the north of Jerusalem, and another called Judea, to the south of Jerusalem. The roots of Israel clearly rest in these hills and valleys that are dotted with almond and fig trees. Nonetheless, there are those who prefer not to blind their eyes with facts.

There is an organization of extreme left political activists in Israel called Peace Now, which has always conveniently ignored these historical facts about the heartland. The name of the organization speaks for itself, for they are willing to give away the entire heartland of Israel immediately, with all of its historical and spiritual significance, in exchange for promises of peace, or pieces of paper that are pretentiously referred to as peace agreements, but are known in the media simply as – peace. In recent years, Peace Now has gained great influence in the shaping of Israeli policy. It apparently doesn't matter to these myopic peace-seekers that the vision of the Palestinian Authority includes control of ALL of Israel. Nor do they seem to care that when the political leaders of the "Palestinians," and their Muslim preachers speak to their own people in Arabic they sing a very different tune, calling for their triumphant return to Jaffa and the Galilee and Haifa, all safely within pre-1967 Israel, and of course their recurring Arabic chant, "With blood and fire we will redeem you O'Jerusalem." Peace with our terrorist enemies has become the Golden Calf of our times, and everyone wants to blindly get on board and sing its praises, whatever the cost.

"...they have eyes, but cannot see; they have ears, but cannot hear..."
(Psalms 115:5-6)

In other words, Judea and Samaria (the West Bank) are not the ultimate targets. And the Arab leaders don't just limit their bold proclamations to Israel and the Jews. In Arabic, they proudly declare, "First we're going to get the Saturday people and then the Sunday people!" Sometimes the terminology is not so polite and the Sunday people (Christians) are simply referred to as "the infidels." All of the leaders of the Arab nations are now Muslim, and the words above are being proclaimed in mosques around the world. The dire ramifications for the entire free world and the hoped for world peace should not be understated.

It should be pointed out that the founder of Islam about fifteen hundred years ago was a man named Mohammed. This Mohammed claimed to be a prophet, but his claims were utterly rejected by all of the Jews and Christians who he came into contact with. As a result of this rejection, he decided to create a new religion and a new god (Allah), to take revenge against those who had rejected him, by essentially proclaiming, "My god is bigger than your god!" The Islamic holy book, the Koran, confirms this:

"Believers, do not seek the friendship of the infidels and those who were given the Book before you, who have made of your religion a jest and a pastime."
(Koran: Sura V: verse 57)

"Shall I tell you who will receive a worse reward from Allah? Those whom Allah has cursed and with whom he has been angry, transforming them into apes and swine, and those who serve the devil."
(Koran: Sura V: verse 60)

In other words, Mohammed was angry at those who rejected his claims of prophecy, so his religion refers to them in terms that anyone who really wants to be "politically correct" should be calling racism or bigotry.

"Allahu Akbar is the call to prayer from the mosques throughout the world. It is also the battle cry of Moslems when they go to war against anyone, even against themselves. The mainline media translates this as 'God is great!' But that's not what it really means. Kebir in Arabic means great. Akbar is diminutive of Kebir, and it means 'greater.' What Moslems are really saying: 'Our god is greater than their god.'" (Avi Lipkin, *Is Fanatic Islam a Global Threat?*, 1996)

Incredibly, the world is filled with both Jews and Christians who fail to see that the threat to the free world is not just from "radical Islam," but from the Islamic mainstream. Just as many in the free world preferred not to risk war to confront the threat of Nazism less than seventy years ago, and to confront the Communist threat just thirty-five years ago, so too, we have many world leaders who are closing their eyes regarding the Islamic threat, which is growing every day, in the mainstream of Islam. Despite his otherwise bold statements after 9/11 about the war on terrorism, even President George W. Bush sounded outright defensive when asked about the Muslim threat as represented by the attack on the World Trade Center:

"The face of terror is not the true faith of Islam. That's not what Islam is all about. Islam is peace."
(U.S. Pres. George Bush, September 17, 2001)

"Take a concept like jihad, which is central to understanding the war on terror, and you hear historians of Islam, religious specialists or others saying that jihad is moral self-improvement - becoming a better colleague; working on behalf of women's rights; working against apartheid. They are generally unwilling to state what it really is, which is warfare that expands Muslim control of land."
(Daniel Pipes, Jerusalem Post, June 9, 2006)

So what gives? Is Islam, as represented by its mainstream governments and spiritual leadership, really a religion of peace? It is certainly no accident that 15 of the 19 bombers who attacked the World Trade Center in New York City were from the "moderate" Islamic Kingdom of Saudi Arabia, the great "friend" of the free world. But most non-Muslim Americans and Europeans prefer to ignore such uncomforting bits of information, because the thought of potential conflict, accompanied by rising oil prices and long gas lines is too painful and scary. Better to put their collective heads in the Middle Eastern sand, ignore the threat, and hope that it will go away.

And so the surreal delusion continues, to the extent that staunch

Muslim terrorists and Holocaust deniers like Yasser Arafat and Mahmoud Abbas, are recognized by Israel and the free world as "peace partners" and in the case of Arafat, given a Noble Peace Prize.

> "He'll put both his arms around you
> You can feel that tender touch of a beast
> You know that sometime Satan come as a man of peace."
> *(Bob Dylan's song, "Man of Peace", 1983)*

It is indeed a bizarre state of affairs when terror leaders are given substantial political and financial support by the American and European governments that claim to be participating in a war against terrorism, often under the guise of "humanitarian aid," with the acquiescence of an Israeli government that longs for acceptance from the nations of the world. In other words, we'll give you (the so-called Palestinians) our land, our water, even our guns; just tell us you want peace! Even the most instinctual sense of pride and self-preservation goes out the window when knowledge of and pride in Israel's heritage is lacking.

As with any symptom, this particular Israeli problem hasn't arisen in a vacuum, but is a product of a valueless Israeli secular educational system. The Israeli educational system is divided into several divisions, each with a different set of goals. The two largest are the public secular and the public religious. In the religious schools, prayer and varied learning of Torah subjects is central, in addition to Math, Hebrew, English, and other subjects; while in the secular division, in which the majority of the current adult population was educated, only the secular subjects are taught. Sadly, the most basic Bible education from a position of faith (as opposed to a nice fairy tale or legend) is usually non-existent in the secular schools of Israel. In this particular socio-religious context, it becomes almost possible to comprehend the government policy of giving away our God-given ancestral Lands, for if one learns the Bible without God, it is robbed of all of its existential depth, and there is little incentive to follow His instructions regarding the Land of Israel, not to mention all of the other commandments. This is the sad reality in Israel today, where a large segment of the population has been educated to be disconnected from its magnificent heritage. Is it any wonder that the average product of such an educational system is literate and often has high-level computer skills, yet can't describe three events in the life of Moses?

"They have dealt treacherously against the Lord, for they have be-gotten strange children." (Hosea 5:7)

It should also come as no surprise to us that many political leaders in Israel today make fateful national decisions based only on pressure from the United States government, desire for political advancement, or even personal corruption. When the fear of man is greater than the fear of the Almighty, His commandments become quaint fairy tales and the whims of world leaders become reality.

"Woe to them that go down to Egypt for help and rely on horses and trust in chariots because they are many and in horsemen because they are exceedingly mighty; But they look not unto the Holy One of Israel...So when the Lord will stretch out His hand, and the helper will stumble and the helped will fall; they will all perish together." (Isaiah 31:1-3)

"Many solicit a ruler's favor, but from the Lord will come judgement." (Proverbs 29:26)

In order to properly understand this ongoing debate, it's also necessary to understand the relatively recent historical context. In 1964, the Palestine Liberation Organization was formed. It consisted of many Arabs who had lived in, or had relatives in, the area that had become the State of Israel. Its leader was the soon to be notorious terrorist Yasser Arafat, who was born in and grew up in Cairo, Egypt. Its clearly stated goal was the destruction of the State of Israel. In 1974, the Arab nations and the PLO met at the ground-breaking Rabat Conference in Morocco, where they again agreed to try to destroy Israel, but this time there was a barely- noticed, but significant change of strategy. No longer would they rely only on "the military struggle." From that point onwards, the Arabs would simultaneously endeavor to wipe out the Jewish State step-by-step through a diplomatic process, in addition to, but not instead of, military means. They would now agree to accept any land that Israel would agree to surrender, rather than insisting on the whole pie all at once. It became known as "the stages plan", a revised two-prong strategy for the ultimate destruction of Israel.

This piece-by-piece approach to the ongoing war against Israel is important for us to remember, because it is relevant to this day, as the world, including Israeli leaders, continue to mistake "piece" for "peace."

In 1993, secret negotiations were held between the PLO and the Israeli government in Oslo, Norway and the so-called peace process was accelerated, the ramifications of which we are suffering from to this day. It soon become known as "the Oslo Peace Process", in which Israel obligated itself to withdraw, as a first step, from the largest cities in Judea, Samaria, and Gaza, with the hint of possible total Israeli withdrawal from the Biblical heartland, an act of foolishness that would put the heavily-populated coastal cities of Israel within nine miles of enemy missiles.

The Oslo Process brought with it an ongoing terror war by the "Palestinians", the Arabs of the Land of Israel, which has killed and wounded many thousands of Jewish Israelis in the last ten years. As a result of the Oslo Agreements, massive quantities of weapons were transferred to the Palestinian Authority, the quasi-government created to cooperate with (but in effect, manipulates) the Israeli government. Substantial amounts of money poured into the P.A. from the United States and European governments, ostensibly for economic projects, but in reality used for the build-up of weapons and ammunition to fuel the ongoing terror war against Israel. The weakness of successive Israeli governments that were either willing to, or eager to withdraw from vital portions of the Land of Israel, only encouraged the Arabs that their war of terror was having its desired effect.

"We may hope for peace, but there is no goodness; for a time of healing, but behold, there is terror." (Jeremiah 8:15)

In the summer of 2000, there was a trilateral meeting of political leaders in the presidential retreat at Camp David, Maryland. There President Clinton hosted then Prime Minister Ehud Barak and P.A. Chairman Yasser Arafat in an attempt to broker an agreement that would ostensibly create peace in the Middle East. At that weeklong summit, which consisted of lots of back-slapping in addition to serious meetings and heavy pressure, Barak offered almost total Israeli withdrawal from all of the territories which God had placed in its hands in the Six Day War of 1967. Shiloh, Hebron, Beth El, even the

Temple Mount in Jerusalem, with all of their rich Biblical history were to be placed in the hands of the enemy that was attacking Israel with greater and greater frequency, and was building an army to do so with greater effectiveness.

Much of the world was surprised that an Israeli leader would surrender so much simply for the promise of peace, which had sadly been heard too many times before. While Barak received much praise in the world media for his "bold move", there were thousands of voices of dissent in Israel and among the many pious Jews from around the world that an Israeli leader would even consider giving up the Temple Mount and the most ancient parts of Jerusalem. There was also respectful, but palpable head-shaking on the part of many evangelical Christians around the world, who couldn't fathom why Israel would be so willing to give up its divine inheritance in the Biblical heartland.

"And they scorned the desirable land and believed not His word."
(Psalms 106:24)

"You make of us an object of strife unto our neighbors, and our enemies laugh amongst themselves." (Psalms 80:7)

At the end of the Camp David Summit, the Arabs surprised all of those Israelis, who had been viewing the world through rose-colored glasses for several years, and had been foolishly proclaiming that peace was at hand. Nobel Peace Prize winning Israeli politician Shimon Peres had even gone so far as to write a book about his myopic vision of an idyllic "New Middle East", in which the Arab world would join with Israel in peace and in the spirit of economic cooperation. Clearly this was not to be, as PLO leader Yasser Arafat rejected Ehud Barak's offer, stormed out of Camp David, and the Palestinian Arabs launched a vicious terror war on all fronts that was of such a magnitude that it shocked, at least temporarily, almost all shades of the Israeli political spectrum. Horrific bus bombings in the cities of Israel, sniper attacks on the roads, and infiltrations into communities in Samaria, Judea, Gaza, and elsewhere in the country became almost daily events. Obviously, the "occupied territories" of the "West Bank" and Gaza were not the only problem. For at least a few moments, the truth became transparent for those who were willing to see, that the problem for the Arab world has never been the "occupied territories" of 1967. No, the problem was, is, and will remain, at least in the foreseeable future, all of the territories captured by Israel in all of the wars, including the 1948 War of Independence, namely, the State of Israel. In short, the very presence of Israel, all of Israel, as a sovereign nation in the Middle East was unacceptable to the descendants of Ishmael.

"And he (Ishmael) will be a wild man; his hand will be against every man, and every man's hand against him..." (Genesis 16:12)

Ehud Barak's other legacy was his decision to unilaterally withdraw all remaining Israeli troops from the buffer zone in Lebanon, also in the year 2000. It was a decision that was well-received by an Israel that had grown tired of the Lebanon morass, where young Israeli soldiers had been forced into defensive mode by their own government. Originally left in Lebanon to prevent rocket and terror attacks on northern Israel, they had often been hit by Hezbollah sniper fire. The demoralized Israeli public, no longer understanding the maxim that the best defense is a good offense, had also been led to believe by the "run for peace" proponents that the only solution to being "sitting ducks" was to run away. And that's what Ehud Barak did, perhaps not realizing that six years later, his decision would come back to haunt him (see Chapter 9).

Back in 1984, when I was still living in New York, I had a friend named Hillel Lieberman. Hillel and I were both already longing to live in Israel. He used to tell me proudly, with a smile and a twinkle in his youthful eyes, that he was going to live in Shechem, a city populated only by several hundred thousand hostile Arabs. Why would a young idealistic Jew choose to live in such a dangerous place?

"Joseph's bones, which the Children of Israel had brought up from Egypt, they buried in Shechem, in the portion of the field that Jacob had acquired from the children of Hamor, the father of Shechem, for a hundred kesitas, and it became a heritage for the children of Joseph." (Joshua 24:32)

The Biblical Joseph, the beloved son of the Patriarch Jacob and first-born son of the Matriarch Rachel, requested before he died that

Fulfillment of a Promise: *Joseph's Tomb in Shechem, ca. 1900*

his bones be taken out of Egypt and carried into the Land of Israel. He was buried many years later in Shechem, where his father had purchased land hundreds of years prior. Joseph was the archetype of the Jew who succeeded in Gentile society, as the only Jew in Egypt, rising to the very highest position possible, just below Pharaoh. Despite all this, while his accomplishments were in Egypt, his heart was in the Land of Israel. His children, Ephraim and Manasseh, became the heads of two of the most important of the tribes, whose portions were in the Biblical heartland of Israel. Joseph's determination to be buried in the Land of Israel, and the determination of the Children of Israel who persisted in carrying his bones with them to their designated burial place, despite their lengthy sojourn in the desert, stands out as a symbol of Israel's yearning for its Land.

Hillel Lieberman had that determination to leave his comfortable home in the United States and move near Joseph's ultimate burial place, where he married and raised a family. He lived with his wife and seven children in Elon Moreh, one of the Jewish communities overlooking Shechem, and every day he would drive down to the small yeshiva (religious seminary) at the site of Joseph's Tomb in Shechem, where he happily learned and taught Torah.

"And Abram passed through the Land as far as the site of Shechem, until Elon Moreh (lit. trans. – the teacher's terebinth, or oak tree)" (Genesis 12:6)

In October of 2000, the Arabs, including soldiers from the Palestinian Authority, went on a violent Sabbath rampage, attacking Israeli soldiers and setting Joseph's Tomb on fire. Rather than defending the holy site and evicting the invaders, then Prime Minister Ehud Barak ordered the Israeli Army to quickly withdraw from the area, and they did so immediately, even leaving an Israeli soldier seriously wounded and bleeding on the battlefield. The soldier eventually died from his wounds. When Hillel heard what was happening in Shechem, he ran out of his community's security gate in a state of panic to get to Joseph's Tomb, not even bringing his gun with him. It was almost as if he had suddenly heard that his children were in danger, so hasty and emotional was his reaction. He was quickly reported missing and it was announced on the news that the police and army were searching for him. His severely mutilated body was found two days later in a cave near Shechem.

The murder of Hillel Lieberman marked the beginning of the worst wave of terror that Israel had ever experienced. Bus bombings in the cities and shootings on the roads of Judea and Samaria became an almost daily occurrence. Some communities were infiltrated at night by Arab terrorists who killed and wounded whoever they could get to, whether man, woman, or child. There were several cases of two parents being shot at and murdered together in their cars, in one case leaving nine young children orphaned. Many parents hesitated to ride together in their cars, for fear of leaving their children orphaned without either parent. Other residents in the Biblical heartland began to drive to work wearing bulletproof vests and even helmets. Still others would only ride on the infrequent bulletproof buses, despite the often inconvenient schedules, which caused them to get to work or return home quite late. On the other hand, others adamantly refused to let the terrorists change their day-to-day routines, and continued driving to work as freely as in the past. Whatever personal decisions people made in this new reality, there was no doubt to anyone that the situation had changed dramatically and that the pioneers in the Biblical

Abandoned By His Brethren Once Again: *After Israeli Prime Minister Ehud Barak ordered the Israel Defense Forces to withdraw, Arab rioters destroyed, burned and desecrated Joseph's Tomb in Shechem.*

heartland would have to once again bear the major daily burden of that challenge.

That unfortunate reality was actualized in June of 2001, when the community of Shiloh, along with most of Israel, was shocked to hear about the murder of the five-month-old baby Yehuda Shoham. He was in a car with his parents, coming back home to Shiloh from a visit to his grandparents' home, when Arab terrorists hurled an enormous rock through the car window, smashing into the infant's head. He was rushed to the hospital in the hope that somehow his life could be saved. After an ongoing vigil of visits and prayers at his hospital bed, he died of his wounds several days later. The shock of this and the many shooting murders on the roads caused great sorrow and nervousness in the heartland communities, but it also created in us a fierce determination to stand firm against the violent attacks of the terrorists and the political pressures of the world, despite the dangers and difficulties that the new situation created for our daily lives, and for the lives of our children. The upsurge in terrorism against Israeli civilians in recent years is a direct and tragic result of the string of naive peace plans and withdrawals through the years that have sent a clear message of Israeli weakness, tiredness, and lack of resolve. Every expulsion of Jewish families, every withdrawal (whether unilateral or arranged), even every handshake with terrorist political leaders sworn to our destruction has spiritual and psychological ramifications in this world. Not only are we sending a message to our enemies that terrorism works, but we are going against the true Spiritual Road Map. For a long time, it has been clear to me that there is only one peace plan or road map that has any chance of working in the Middle East and that is the road map of Abraham, Isaac and Jacob; a peace plan that is based on the historical promises made to our forefathers. The tragic results of the man-made peace plans of recent years have only reinforced my beliefs, and I will continue to emphasize the basic Biblical principles that should guide our fateful decisions. There is no doubt that any peace plan that ignores the unambiguous instructions of the Bible is doomed to failure, and will only bring more terrorism.

"...you shall not seal a covenant with the inhabitants of this land...but you have not obeyed my voice." (Judges 2:2)

Many years ago, when I was still living in New York, I used to learn Torah several times a week with an elderly rabbi. It was a special relationship, in which this wise old man with a long white beard, who had lived through persecution and the Holocaust and was then nearing the end of his life, happily gave of his time to teach me the basics of Judaism.

"From wise elders I gain understanding, because I have guarded Your precepts." (Psalms 119:100)

One day, after having learned with him for a few years, he greeted me with his usual smile, but when we sat down, with our Bibles in front of us, his expression turned serious. He stared at me for close to a minute without saying a word, and then spoke the following words:

"David, I want to talk to you about the most important thing that a Jew can do." Again, close to a minute of silence, then, with pleading, piercing eyes filled with tears, he spoke again: "The most important thing that a Jew can do is to sacrifice for the People of Israel in the Land of Israel." Instead of giving a more typical lesson that day, he continued in this vein, explaining that by sacrificing for His People, a Jew is actually sacrificing for the God of Israel, because Israel is so special to Him (see Zechariah 2:12), and what we do for His People we are actually doing for Him. He reiterated this point again, and concluded by emphasizing that one should not be afraid to suffer for the God of Israel.

Little did I know it at that time, but some twelve years later, I would have that advice put to the test. The escalating terror war on Israel, and in particular on the residents of the Biblical heartland, became a catalyst for the most dramatic change in my life and in the lives of my wife and children.

Chapter Eight
On God's Wings

"Three things are acquired through great suffering: Torah,
The Land of Israel, and the World to Come." (Talmud: Brachot: 5)

When meeting people from outside of Israel, or even Israelis from perhaps less dangerous parts of the country, I have often been confronted with a barrage of questions concerning the ever-present danger on the roads and how we go on with our day-to-day lives. The question is almost always asked: Don't you ever consider moving to a safer place, where you don't have to worry about your day-to-day safety and the safety of your children? Why live in an area where you are vastly outnumbered by Arabs who don't want you there, where most of the world doesn't want you to be, and where they are launching terror attacks against you almost daily?

The fact is, we don't think about these questions much. People go on with their lives without thinking daily about alternatives, but more importantly, if people would flee under pressure from the terrorists' bullets and bombs, then it would be clear who has won the battle. To surrender to evil is a dangerous precedent that the free world should refuse to allow, and that should never be agreed to.

Despite the new reality of the intensive post-Oslo Accords terrorism that cast a long shadow on the lives of the residents living in the heartland of Israel, there was always the unstated feeling of, "Well, it's not going to happen to me!" No one would say that aloud, but the feeling was always resting a bit below the surface. This was, to some extent, a case of putting one's head in the sand, but the feeling of denial was very real among many people at that time, despite the increasing news reports of terror attacks, some of them frighteningly close to home.

The left-wing secular-dominated media in Israel, whether print, radio, or television, often played down the suffering of "the settlers", as if our wounds were self-inflicted, by our choice to live in the heartland, a specious argument at best, since the grassroots efforts to build up Judea and Samaria were quietly encouraged by almost every Israeli government. Nonetheless, the media pounding has continued unabated for many years. How could we live in a region where the Arabs vastly outnumber us? This has been the refrain of the media's song, as well as that of many left of center Israeli politicians. Such a position has ignored the basic fact that Judea and Samaria always have been and remain a microcosm of the State of Israel as a whole, for what people in their right minds would go to live in a state the size of New Jersey, with just five million other Jews, surrounded by hundreds of millions of hostile Muslims who live in a land mass five hundred times the size of the State of Israel? The demographic argument also has ignored the fact that the Jewish population in Judea and Samaria tends to have large families and is growing at a rate faster than that of the Arabs. Nonetheless, the stereotypical image of "the religious settler" created by the media has not been a complimentary one, and those in the heartland have been made the favorite scapegoat for most of the ills afflicting Israeli society. Yes, much of the general public was led to believe by the constant image-baiting, that the settlers in Judea and Samaria were the cause of most of Israel's problems, from poverty to Arab hostility. In reality, those who had chosen to live in Israel's heartland were, for the most part, sincere, family-oriented idealists valiantly redeeming the heartland against all odds, including terrorism, political isolation, and international pressure. Many had also undoubtedly moved there for quality of life reasons, as most people do in other parts of Israel and other parts of the world, but that was certainly no crime, nor a reason to demonize an entire geographic segment of the Israeli population.

The terrorism on the roads increased drastically after the failed Camp David Summit in the year 2000. Since the signing of the Oslo Accords in 1993, every sign of Israeli weakness had brought on a noticeable increase in terror attacks. The media focused on the terrible bus bombings in the cities, but the residents of the Israeli heartland, known in the media only as "the settlers," were on the receiving end of the terrorists' bullets. The terrorists, using their Kalashnikov assault rifles, launched daily shooting attacks on the residents of the heartland communities, but much of the media ignored the trauma of the rapidly increasing number of terror victims in Judea, Samaria, and Gaza. By 2001, every commute to work or school had become a

perilous adventure for the mothers, fathers, and children of the heartland. As I mentioned earlier, many residents drove to work wearing
bulletproof vests and some even helmets, while many others stopped
commuting in their cars altogether, preferring the bulletproof, if sometimes inconvenient buses. Still others refused to change their way of
life, and insisted on traveling to work in their own cars, either with a
gun, or with no protection at all.

In short, everyone adapted to the new reality in his or her own
way, but to everyone it was clear that we had entered a new phase in
the struggle for the Land of Israel. Most of the residents of Samaria,
Judea, and Gaza developed a renewed spirit of camaraderie, as often
happens when an entire segment of a population is under attack. This
was a population that believed in the justness of its mission, and its
God-given right to the Land and wasn't prepared to allow the terrorists and their collaborators to achieve their violent goals.

The shootings on the roads finally hit home for my own family
in a very personal way several years ago on the last night of Hannukah.
That afternoon, I had experienced a terrible toothache, so I decided
that I had to go to my dentist in Jerusalem. I decided to take at least
one or two of our children with me, to make it easier for my wife,
who was busy at home that day. I asked my then seven-year-old daughter Avital if she wanted to take the ride with me, but she said she
wanted to stay home in Shiloh and play with her friends. When I
asked my then five-year-old, Michal, she responded by asking, "Are
there Arabs there?" I calmly told her that yes there were some Arabs
in Jerusalem, but that they wouldn't bother us, and that there was
nothing to be afraid of. She remained unconvinced and decided to
stay at home. My three-year-old son Reuven, known to everyone as
Ruby, had no say in the matter, so he came with me to Jerusalem.
Much to my surprise, the dentist could find no cavity or any problem
in my mouth. Ruby and I went out for lunch, and then for haircuts.
Just past 5.30 P.M. on this dark winter night, we began our ride home
to Shiloh in our car, Ruby sitting happily behind me, safely buckled
into his toddler seat.

We rode north on the historic, hilly, but dark country road which
(as we discussed earlier) is called by the historic name the Road of the
Patriarchs, or by the modern name of Road 60. We were about half-
way home when I heard on the radio news at the top of the hour that
an Israeli driver had just been shot and wounded in a different part of

Samaria.

Exactly at that moment, there was a sudden hail of bullets on my car. The car radio went dead, as did the car's engine. I saw the sparks from what appeared to be four bullets zooming past me, as the car was slowly coasting down the hill. The bullets had tracers on them, so they appeared as four orange sparks whizzing past, perhaps two inches in front of my eyes. Then I felt a terrible pain, like a concentrated ton of bricks crashing into my left leg, and the blood started gushing out fiercely, like an open fire hydrant. At that point, I remembered that I had my toddler sitting in back of me in the baby seat and I frantically turned to him and asked him, "Ruby, are you okay?" He just stared straight ahead. His eyes were wide open. His mouth was wide open. He looked like he was trying to cry, but no sounds were coming out. I didn't see any blood, so I assumed that he was just in shock. I quickly tried to start the ignition, but with no success, shifting gears from drive to park to neutral and back again, and the terrorists were still shooting! Finally, on the fourth or fifth attempt, the car started, and it started smoothly, as if there had never been a problem. I slammed my right foot on the gas pedal and drove 110 miles an hour to reach the next community, called Ofra, in the hope of finding an ambulance there, knowing all along that I could collapse from loss of blood at any moment.

The truth is, I didn't think about what to do at all. There really was no time to think about a plan of action. I was operating totally from instinct, as if my actions were being dictated by remote from above.

"Even when I walk in the valley of darkness, I will fear no evil for you are with me." (Psalms 23:4)

As I drove speedily, frantically forward, my left leg was pounding as the blood flowed out, and I reached down to touch it as I was driving, but all I could feel was blood, which my hand was covered with. I repeatedly tried, unsuccessfully, to reach the security services on the special car radio designed for that purpose.

I reached Ofra in two and a half minutes (normally a five minute drive), opened the car window as I reached the area of the security gate, and started shouting to the guard who was standing in the security booth to quickly call for an ambulance. When the guard didn't seem to respond, a young woman who had been sitting on the side of the road started jumping up and down, shouting," Ambulance! Ambulance! Don't you hear?" At that moment, everyone who was within sound's reach came running over, one of whom was the gas station attendant, who ran up to the car shouting, "I'm also a medic", and immediately ripped off my shirt and wrapped up my leg to try to stop the blood flow. He gave me his cell phone, and said, "Here, call your wife", but my hand was shaking so much that I couldn't dial. He dialed the number for me, wrapping up my leg with one hand and dialing the phone number with the other, and then handing me the phone. I told my wife, "I've been shot in the leg; they'll be taking me to the hospital when the ambulance comes, and Ruby is okay." She assured me that she would somehow get to the hospital, no simple task at night, with no car and fear on the roads. Just then, the ambulance arrived. A medic from the ambulance ran to the car and started to take my son out of the car. I urged him to let Ruby stay in the car, and told him that Ruby was just in shock and needed to be with me. He ignored my request, pulled my toddler out of the car, and dashed to the ambulance, shouting, "He's also been shot. He's been shot in the neck!"

A Pool of Blood: After a nearly 120 mph race to the ambulance in Ofra, the car went dead again in Ofra, had to be towed to the police station in Beth El, and from there to the car garage in Jerusalem. To this day, no one has been able to explain why it went dead, started, and again went dead.

At that moment, my entire mood changed. The composure that had enabled me to get to the ambulance fell apart, due to a mixture of emotional pain and anger. I could easily deal with my own physical wounds, but why did the terrorists need to shoot my three-year-old? This innocent soul with the care-free smile could never hurt a fly. That's who they needed to carefully aim for with their Kalashnikov tracer bullets? Ruby was quickly wrapped with bandages around his head and neck. An oxygen mask was put on his face and we were both whisked into the ambulance on stretchers and laid in the ambu-

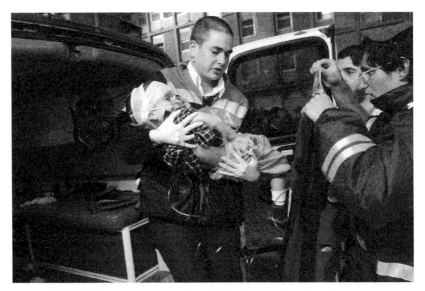

Bandaged Baby in Good Hands: *Ruby being taken from the ambulance to the emergency room at Hadassah Ein Karem Hospital.*

lance, to be taken to one of the hospitals in Jerusalem.

I later found out that a bullet had gone into Ruby's head, in the place where the skull meets with the neck, causing a skull fracture and internal bleeding in his cerebellum, the back part of the brain. After what seemed like an endlessly long ride during which Ruby had difficulty breathing at times and the oxygen needed to be adjusted, we reached the hospital in Jerusalem, and were taken into separate emergency rooms. After about ten minutes in the emergency room, one of the doctors told me, "We are going to have to operate on both you and your son within the half hour, probably the first of several operations, but there's someone here who wants to see you." My first thought was that the Prime Minister had come to visit, or possibly one of the government ministers. Surely at some point, I thought, they would stand up and take at least the minimal responsibility for their inability or unwillingness to protect the country's citizens! A hospital visit to a wounded toddler would at least demonstrate a minimal amount of concern. But this was not to be.

"And all of the elders of the city...shall answer and say: Our hands have not shed this blood, and our eyes did not see." (Deuteronomy 21:6-7)

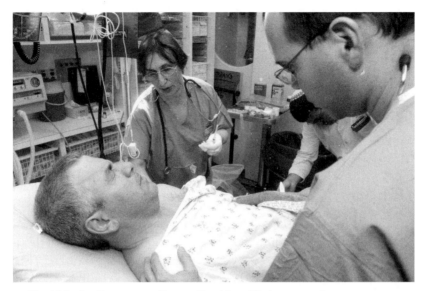

David in the Emergency Room: *David and Ruby were taken to separate emergency rooms, before their first operations that were soon to come.*

A man walked in who I had never seen before, introduced himself as the public relations director for Hadassah Ein Karem hospital, and said, "I just want you to know that you are the 1,000th victim of terror to be hospitalized in this hospital in the past year and a half." Knowing that there are several large hospitals in Israel, it was quite a statement. Anyhow, I wasn't sure how to respond to this dubious little honor that I had just had bestowed upon me. Was I supposed to get a prize? It was an almost surreal comic moment in the middle of the trauma. He went on to tell me that the media people were massing outside the emergency room to interview and photograph the 1,000th victim of terrorism, but if I preferred, he would keep them away to protect our privacy. At that moment, all of the frustration that

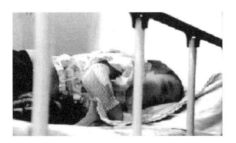

Ruby asleep in the Children's Intensive Care Ward: *He was sleeping most of the day, due to internal bleeding in his cerebellum. When he was awake, he didn't remember his siblings or friends.*

had been building up over the previous years of terrorism against Israeli civilians came to the fore, and I said, "No, there is nothing private about this. You can bring them in." And I've been telling this story ever since those first twenty-four hours in the hospital, where we ended up spending several very physically and emotionally exhausting weeks.

For several weeks, I was allowed to be taken in my wheelchair just once a day to visit Ruby in the intensive care unit of the children's ward, which was in an adjacent building. He was sleeping most of the day and couldn't even lift himself up in bed. He had almost total memory loss, not even remembering his siblings or friends. This, I later learned, was a result of the psychological trauma, and his memory would gradually return after months of psychological therapy. In short, these weeks were agonizing. My exhausted but indefatigable wife, Lisa, was shuttling back and forth daily from our home in Shiloh to the hospital, an hour and a half away, and often spending the night in the hospital with Ruby, when she was able to arrange someone to take her place at home, so that our other children would be taken care of as well. Lisa is the quintessential modern Jewish woman, accomplished at work, but fiercely devoted to her husband and children, and of course capable of doing five things at one time. I don't know how we would have managed to get through this difficult period without her holding things together.

"Many women have amassed achievement, but you surpassed them all." (Proverbs 31:29)

After Ruby returned home several weeks later, he would often wake up hysterically screaming at night, usually calling for his mother. At those painful moments, I was the last person he wanted to see, and when I would hobble over to him using my walker to get to him, he would scream even louder. The emotional trauma was a greater challenge for us than was the physical. It was painful for me to see Ruby essentially crying out for help, yet not being emotionally capable of receiving my assistance.

As I mentioned earlier, the bullet from a Kalashnikov assault rifle had entered Ruby's head in the place where the skull meets the neck, causing a fracture and internal bleeding in the cerebellum, the back section of the brain, which regulates sleep, balance, and other

B'klyn-born settler and son wounded

By Uri Dan in Jerusalem and Marsha Kranes in New York

A Brooklyn-born teacher and his 3-year-old son were wounded when Palestinians fired on their car as they headed to their home on the Israeli-occupied West Bank.

"They started shooting at us, a lot of shooting," David Rubin, 44, said of the Monday night ambush.

One of the slugs slammed into Rubin's leg; another hit his son, Ruby, in the back of his neck, narrowly missing his spine.

The two were returning to the Jewish settlement of Shilo after a day's outing in Jerusalem when Palestinians opened fire from a passing car.

Ruby went into immediate shock and didn't answer his father's shouts.

Rubin, who was losing blood, battled pain and increasing weakness to keep driving.

When he finally reached the nearest settlement, Ofra, "he opened the car door, fell out and called for help," said Eitan, his 14-year-old stepson.

A local man rushed the Rubins to a Jerusalem hospital.

"My father is OK. He just has a hole in his leg," Eitan reported. "My brother is more serious. When we visited him yesterday, he didn't recognize me or my sisters. He only recognized my mother."

בן 3 נפצע עם אביו בפיגוע ירי ביו"ש

The Day After

These were some of the headlines from the morning after the attack. The Hebrew one reads, "Three-Year-Old Son Wounded With His Father in Shooting Attack in Samaria."

THE JERUSALEM
POST
www.jpost.com

LXIX, NUMBER 21067   TUESDAY, DECEMBER 18, 2001 • 3 TEVET 5762 • 3 SHAWAL 1422   NIS 6.00 (EILAT NIS 5.10)

3 wounded in terrorist ambushes

Terror Victim Recalls Attack Near Ofra

'It was not one miracle that saved us, it was a number of miracles'

It was just after 6 p.m. Monday, when Brooklyn-born Shilo resident David Rubin was driving home from a day in Jerusalem with his 3-year-old son ... when his ...

was being shot at, and the car was crawling down the hill," he said.

In a panic, he repeatedly hit the red ...

Three-year-old Shilo boy Ruby Rubin, shot with his father David by drive-by terrorists last night near Ofra, arrives at Jerusalem's Hadassah-University Hospital in Ein Kerem.

physiological functions. He also experienced vision problems, a result of damage to the optic nervous system caused by the wound in the back of his head. This necessitated another operation several months later. These were just some of the physical hurdles my little boy had to overcome, but as I said the emotional challenges were much greater and more painful for all of us. I've already referred to the sleep problems and the nightmares and the lost sense of emotional security.

During the weeks after the attack, I spoke about the experience constantly, whether in the media, or with the many friends and family who came to visit or called up from overseas. This was for me a form of post-trauma therapy. My young child didn't have that verbal option, so the emotional frustration and pain had to find another outlet, a means of release. A few weeks after being released from the hospital, while I was still at home on disability, Ruby stood inside a large toy bus. "It's an ambulance," he said. I suddenly realized that this could be a good opportunity for some play therapy, so I responded, "Really? Who's in the ambulance?" There were two dolls inside. Ruby said, "It's a baby and he's been shot! Arabs shot him." I asked him, "Who's the other doll?" Ruby answered," It's his Abba (father). He's been shot in the leg."

Despite my many years of experience working with young children and learning about child psychology, I was amazed and moved to tears at what I was hearing. No, Ruby did not have the emotional or verbal capability, nor the maturity, to sit and discuss what had happened to him, but here he was, explicitly reliving the trauma through play. I pulled out all the press clippings that I had, as well as get-well pictures from his little friends, and photos related to the attack. With Ruby at my side, I carefully put them in an album. That really opened him up, and to the extent that he was able to, we discussed the attack. For the next several months, he was fascinated with that album, especially the emergency room pictures. It took a couple of months from that point, but we found a good post-trauma emotional therapy program at one of the hospitals in Jerusalem. There was no treatment program closer to home, so we traveled there by buses once a week for several months, which wasn't easy for either of us at the time, but compared to what we had gone through...

Looking back, I think the most important thing is to examine what we have learned from the experience. We Jews believe that everything that happens, occurs for a good reason. In other words, good

Psalms Under Attack: *A bullet went completely through the Book of Psalms, but it was still readable.*

things should come out of every seemingly bad experience. The morning after the attack, the Chief Rabbi of Shiloh, Elchanan Bin Nun, whose 19-year-old son had been killed in a terror attack just three years prior, came to the hospital to visit us. Approaching my bed, his first words to me were, "David, I'm sure that you've started counting miracles." The truth is that I hadn't, but as I started to think about it, the thought was overwhelming. First of all, I was shot in my left leg, even though they were shooting from the right side, which enabled me to drive my automatic car to get away from the bullets and reach the ambulance. Secondly, the head of the intensive care unit of the children's ward had told us, "You don't know how blessed you are, because if that bullet had gone just one millimeter deeper into your son's neck, it would have hit his brain stem, and he could have been dead on the spot." Those were just two of the miracles that stood out in my mind, but there were others. The bullet that had ripped apart my leg missed the bone and the main nerves. It felt like there wasn't much tissue left, and the plastic surgery that I underwent several weeks after must have been a challenge for the capable surgeon (then Professor, now Knesset member Aryeh Eldad) that performed the operation. All of these were what we call hidden miracles, the kind of miracles that we have to look for, because they can sometimes be explained as well in human terms. However, there are also revealed miracles, the kinds that are just so obvious that we can't even attempt to logically explain them away in human terms. On my fifth or sixth day in the hospital, I got a phone call: "Hi David, this is the car mechanic. I just want you to know that we have the car. There are holes all over the car and we've already started ordering parts and..." At that point, I cut him off, saying, "I don't care about the car. I haven't even thought about the car. I'm allowed to be pushed in a wheelchair once a day for a half an hour to visit my son in the intensive care ward. He's lost his memory, sleeps most of the day, can't even sit up in bed, and doesn't remember his siblings, and you're calling me about a car?

To this he responded, "David, I'm not really calling to tell you the details of which parts we're ordering, or even how much it will cost (a lot). There really is only one reason why I'm calling you at this time. I have to ask you one question." Then there was an eerie silence for a few seconds, before he asked me, "Why can't we start the car?" When he said these words, a chill went down my back, and I shook my head in disbelief. I knew that the car engine had gone dead after the bullets hit the car, and I tried to start the car four or five times, shifting gears while they were still shooting, until the car finally started without any hesitation. I distinctly remember driving that car almost 120 miles an hour to get away from the bullets and to get to an ambulance. And now the mechanic was telling me that the car had to be towed from Ofra, where the ambulance was, to the police station in Beth El, and from there it had to be towed to the car garage in Jerusalem, where the mechanic was now telling me that he doesn't understand why he can't start the car! After almost twenty years as a believer in the God of Israel, I was suddenly confronted with a revealed miracle that had occurred on that fateful night in front of my eyes. We were simply carried on the wings of God to get us to that ambulance! There was just no other way for a reasonable person to explain it. Yes, it's true that there were 45 bullet holes throughout the car, but to this day, no one, including the car mechanic, has been able to explain to me why the car went dead or why it eventually started to get us to that ambulance and then went dead again.

The truth is that I have always been a bit of a skeptic about personal miracle stories. In the world of the religious, there are some

Under His Mother's Watchful Eye*: Apparently fully recovered, Ruby happily takes part in Open School Day in his second-grade class, but for his parents, the trauma of a wounded toddler is never completely finished.*

individuals who will literally believe anything that sounds spiritual, to the extent that anyone can tell a tall tale that sounds good, and there will always be someone to believe it. While such desperate need to believe anything may indeed exist, my personal encounter with terror forced me to confront my own rational cynicism. Many years ago, when I was a young adult and a self-proclaimed atheist, my father, of blessed memory (who my son Ruby was named after), once attempted to break through my cynicism by saying, "David, the world is just too amazing. There has to be something greater than us." I ignored him then, and even ridiculed what I considered to be his simplistic view of the world, as opposed to what I considered to be my rational, modern, scientific perspective. Years later, when I started to explore theology from an intellectual basis, I realized that there was no real conflict between science and religion, and that in many ways it was hard to understand the wonders of the universe without the existence of the Creator. Nonetheless, my skeptic's doubts about miracle stories continued, even into my religiously-observant years.

All that changed after my little son Ruby and I were confronted with death, and experienced miracles that defied my stubbornly rational outlook. I could no longer be a skeptic. I was totally humbled by the experience and I thank God every day for giving me the opportunity to directly feel His presence in this world. Since that fateful night, I've told people, usually with tears welling up in my eyes, that I feel thankful to have gone through the experience. I'm often greeted with incredulous expressions of surprise, but I am indeed grateful to have felt the holy presence of the Almighty in my, in our lives.

"Examine me, O Lord, and test me; scrutinize my intellect and my heart. For your kindness is before my eyes, and I have walked in your truth." (Psalms 26:2-3)

Like others who have gone through traumas, I've at times felt perhaps irrational guilt, and have asked myself the question of why we survived the attack and experienced God's miracles, when so many other wonderful people who we knew weren't so fortunate. Why did the King of kings decide to save this lowly servant and his young son, as opposed to the many good people we knew who were brutally murdered?

"Who may ascend the mountain of God, and who may stand in the place of His sanctity?" (Psalms 24:3)

Just taking a brief walk in my neighborhood in Shiloh, we come to the house of the Yerushalmi family, whose 17-year-old son Shmuel was killed in a bus bombing. Several houses further down the block lived Shmuel's friend, 17-year-old Avi Sutton, murdered by terrorists who killed Avi and several other classmates who had been playing on or near their high school basketball court. On that same street is the Kessler family, immigrants from the United States, whose 19-year-old granddaughter Gila Sara was also killed in a bus bombing. Just around the corner is the Shoham family, whose five-month-old baby Yehuda was killed by a rock thrown at his head as he and his parents were driving back from a visit to his grandparents' house. He was resting comfortably in his infant seat when the car was ambushed and the poor baby's fragile skull was smashed. The doctors tried valiantly to revive him, but he died of his wounds after a several day vigil in the hospital's intensive care unit. Walk down the hill from the murdered baby's home and you come to the Apter family, whose son Noam, was in the kitchen of his yeshiva (religious seminary), which combines military service with religious studies. He and three other fellow students were preparing the Sabbath meal for all the other boys who were sitting in the adjacent dining hall. Suddenly, two terrorists from the Islamic Jihad terror organization burst into the kitchen, shooting and wounding Noam and the others. Before Noam fell dead on the floor, he reached out and locked the door to the dining hall and threw away the key, thereby saving the lives of close to one hundred boys in the dining hall. These are only a few examples of the many children of Shiloh who have been killed or wounded by the fanatical Islamic terrorism that we are all facing.

After seeing all this suffering, and after several operations, many doctors' visits, and months of psychological therapy for my son, I decided that I had to do something for the children of Shiloh, who have suffered so much. It is not an exaggeration to say that there is not one child in Shiloh who does not have a parent or a sibling or a friend or a neighbor or a teacher who has been killed or wounded in a terror attack, and they have ALL been traumatized to varying degrees. When one sees the happy faces of the children in the schools here, it's difficult to see the trauma and anxiety that lies below the surface, but it's there. After weighing the logistics for some time, I decided to establish the Shiloh Israel Children's Fund, to support educational, recreational, and therapeutic projects for the children of Shiloh and its surrounding communities. This is my way of thanking God for saving my son's life, by trying to restore a healthy and happy childhood for all of the children. It is also my response to the terrorists, whose hope was certainly to scare us all away from our homes here in the heartland of Israel. My response to them is a positive one, that we are going to stay and grow and build for the next generation. The communities of Gush Shiloh, the Shiloh bloc of communities, and the other communities in Samaria have been blessed with many children, and it is through them that the future of Israel, and indeed, the world, will be determined. The optimism of those who have chosen to live on the front lines of the struggle for the Land of Israel is something to see. Despite the constant terror attacks, threats from the world, and threats and abuse from our own misguided government, the planting and building and educating of the next generation continues.

"And these words, which I command to you today, shall be upon your heart. You shall teach them diligently to your children and you shall speak of them when you sit in your home, while you walk in the street, when you lie down, and when you rise up." (Deuteronomy 6:6-7)

The Jewish people around the world have always been admired for their emphasis on educating the young, but the Israeli secular school system has turned that emphasis upside down by sending the children home from school at 12 noon every day. While in many schools (especially those with a religious emphasis), the parents pay extra so that their children can go to school until 1, 2, or 3 o'clock, the fact remains that the government has placed its priorities contrary to Jewish tradition by not focusing on the children.

It was clear to me that I had to overcome the trauma that we and so many others had experienced, to put our main focus on helping the children. By doing so, we would not just be easing their suffering and stress from the pain of terrorism, but would be providing future leadership for the nation of Israel. The children of the heartland, despite the many obstacles placed in their path, are growing up learning to be proud Jews, who are being raised with a firm knowledge of who they are, where they come from, and to Whom they will have to answer when their time has come.

They are also growing up with another important value, that there are some things worth fighting for. It says in the Talmud that there are three things that are acquired through great suffering: Torah, the Land of Israel, and the World to Come. The children of the heartland are learning this in the holy books, but they are also being raised with this value deep in their hearts. As the great rabbi, known simply as the Vilna Gaon (Genius) wrote, when people have suffered for any of those three treasures, they become an integral part of their spiritual essence. It is for these and similar reasons that I feel greatly optimistic about the future of Israel, despite all of the barriers in our path.

Chapter Nine

Speaking Out

"Say little and do a lot"   (Ethics of the Fathers 1:15)

In the previous chapter, I described that moment in the hospital emergency room when the public relations director told me that I was the one-thousandth victim of terrorism to be hospitalized there in the previous year and a half. He informed me that the media was massing outside the door waiting to interview the one-thousandth victim of terror. He quickly assured me that he would protect my privacy and that of my young son and that he would keep the news people away. My immediate reaction and response was that there was nothing private about the terror attack on us. The bullets that entered Ruby's neck and my leg could have easily hit another father and son or mother and daughter coming home from Jerusalem that night. My philosophy regarding speech has always been that we can learn a lot more by listening and doing than by speaking, and that there is no reason to speak unnecessarily. Nonetheless, for reasons that I couldn't quite explain at that time, I had suddenly been placed in a situation where words and action go hand in hand. I remembered what the Holocaust survivor and author Elie Wiesel once stated so eloquently, that one who has been through a trauma, through a personal test if you will, has the duty to tell the tale. It was clear to me that there was nothing private about what had happened to us, and that if one has the ability to speak out, he has an obligation to do so.

After Ruby and I were wounded, I felt as if a tremendous sense of responsibility, even divine imperative had been placed on my lap, and when I got phone calls in the succeeding days, weeks, and months asking me to speak to various radio, television, and print media, as well as speaking in other settings, I knew that I couldn't remain silent. I had to speak out about the trauma that we had suffered and the miracles that we were privileged to experience, as well as to discuss the lessons to be learned from our experience and to apply them to the current situation in Israel. But even that wasn't enough. The feeling of obligation that I felt stemmed from the guilt feelings that I referred to in the previous chapter, the "Why me?" syndrome. It wasn't our personal experience that I was speaking about, but the experience of all of those children who didn't survive, who remained wounded, or who were emotionally scarred.

I decided that rather than "just" speaking to audiences and to the media, that I needed to turn the evil that was done to us into something good for all of the children in Shiloh, who have been so traumatized by the ongoing Islamic terror war against innocent Israeli civilians. I truly felt that God had presented me with an opportunity and a challenge that couldn't be missed. After many months of trying to decide about the logistics and the best way to start such a project, I established the Shiloh Israel Children's Fund (S.I.C.F.) in 2004, as an outgrowth of this desire to deliver both a message of faith and optimism to people around the world, and to make a real difference in these children's lives. My goal was and is to support educational, recreational, and therapeutic projects for the traumatized children in the heartland of Israel. The main focus of S.I.C.F. at this time is on the children from the communities of Gush Shiloh. (For more information, see the Appendix)

A Project for Israel and the World

Many years ago, I went to a synagogue in Manhattan to hear a speaker from Israel, the then Defense Minister in the Israeli government, Ariel Sharon. At that time, he had not yet adopted the defeatist "We're tired of fighting" attitude. He was respected as a strong advocate for settling the entire Land of Israel, and was a symbol of pride for Jews around the world. One of the last things he said to this predominantly Jewish audience was (I am paraphrasing), "I want to invite all of you to participate in this great project called Israel. The State of Israel is not just a project for the Israelis, but a great Jewish project, and every Jew, wherever he is, has an important role to play."

At that time, I thought this was a wonderful declaration of inclusion, and it seemed to be a deeply-held belief of Mr. Sharon's. However, twenty-five years have passed since that day, and I've seen all of the foolish peace plans and road maps gradually being adopted by more and more of the irresponsible Israeli politicians, including Mr. Sharon, who had once been one of the great builders of Zion. During his tenure as Prime Minister, he took that trend one step further. In the summer of 2005, he carried out a policy of unilateral withdrawal and eviction of thousands of innocent Jewish men, women, and children from their homes, a policy which sent shockwaves throughout the country, as it caused terrible division in the Land. These families were mainly from the Gush Katif area of the Gaza Strip and a few communities of Northern Samaria. Gush Katif was an idyllic bloc of communities built along a stretch of previously unpopulated sand dunes and beaches. Since shortly after the Six-Day War in 1967, Jews had been returning to this area, establishing beautiful communities with strong religious values. The new refugees were the same people who had created magnificent fruit and vegetable hothouses, all with the encouragement of successive governments, but who had suffered daily rocket and shooting attacks on their communities for several years. The stated goal of Sharon's so-called Disengagement Plan was to create a more secure Israel. The results were the opposite as the enemy was, in effect, brought closer to our cities and encouraged to attack by the perception of Israeli weakness. Just as the unilateral Israel retreat from Lebanon six years earlier had encouraged Hezbollah that time was on their side, the unilateral retreat from Gaza sent an identical message. No one can say that the warnings weren't there well ahead of time. Then Military Chief of Staff Moshe Yaalon had criticized the plan many months before its implementation, warning that it would "grant a supportive wind to terrorism." Not only were his warnings ignored, but he was fired from his position for privately voicing his professional opinion to Sharon (see Israel National News, February 16, 2005).

This is not the context to get into former Prime Minister Ariel Sharon's personal or other motives (see Chapter Ten) for his sudden change from one of the greatest supporters of settlement in Judea, Samaria, and Gaza to its destroyer. What is clear, however, is that his political flip-flop did not stem from humanitarian concerns, as these families, many of whom had lived in those areas for two and three generations, were forcibly evicted from their homes, and sent to live for many months, at last count for over a year, in temporary locations, often unlivable and hundreds of miles from their former homes and places of employment. In some 80% of the cases, the former residents of Gaza lost their jobs, most of which had been eliminated by the destruction of the many educational institutions, factories, stores, and greenhouses that had been destroyed along with their homes. The security result of this "bold" move known as disengagement, for which Israel received polite applause from around the world, was Kassam rockets falling on the south of the country on the cities of Sderot and Ashkelon, Katyushas on the north of the country, and increased terrorism of other forms, including shootings, kidnappings, and bombings in the central regions. In the midst of all the fighting, hardly anyone in the media pointed out that the great Israeli panacea, the security wall/fence which was hastily erected through the center of the Land of Israel, had been exposed as a paper tiger, a defensive placebo only suitable for a people of little faith.

"And the righteous person shall live by his faith." (Habakkuk 2:4)

"Faith, in its most sublime function, provides man with
a level of courage that he could not otherwise achieve."
(Rabbi A.Y. Kook, Midot HaRe'iyah, Emunah)

As we've already pointed out, the much-acclaimed "disengagements" from Lebanon, from Gaza, and from the other now autonomous areas of the Palestinian Authority have proven to be anything but that. In fact, they have resulted in greater entanglement with our enemies of the Palestinian Authority, now led by the Hamas Islamic terror organization, and with the overt cooperation of Hezbollah, Al Qaeda, Syria and the Ayatollahs of Iran, as the range of their rockets grows greater and greater, and the fire of their snipers becomes more frequent. Yet much of the world is still sleeping. As the leaders of Iran and the terror groups call for the annihilation of Israel and the West, the Western leaders, especially those in Europe, praise those who seek the destruction of Israel and the West.

"In the region there is of course a country such as Iran –
a great country, a great people and a great civilization which is
respected and which plays a stabilizing role in the region."
*(French Foreign Minister
Philippe Douste-Blazy, Haaretz, July 31, 2006)*

Graffiti on the Wall: *Loosely translated: "Beyond these walls of fear, the People of Israel lives!" The graffiti on the far right simply says "Ghetto." Both are of course referring to the defeatist mentality that has caused this great nation to retreat beyond concrete walls, similar to those that surrounded the Jewish ghettos in Holocaust-era Europe.*

"The real cure for the conflict is elimination of the Zionist regime..."

(Iranian President Mahmoud Ahmadinejad, Jordan Times, August 4, 2006)

"These people are stark-raving mad, but there is a method to their madness, just like Hitler. If Israel disappeared from the face of the earth, it would only make them move faster."

(Former Prime Minister Binyamin Netanyahu, Jerusalem Post, August 11, 2006)

"Oh Muslims everywhere, I call on you to fight and become martyrs in the war against the Zionists and the Crusaders...It is Jihad for the sake of God and will last until (our) religion prevails from Spain to Iraq."

(Al Qaeda Deputy Leader Ayman al-Zawahiri, Aljazeera, July 27, 2006)

In the summer of 2006, six years year after the Israeli flight from

Lebanon, for which then Prime Minister Ehud Barak had received nearly universal international praise, and exactly one year after Sharon's retreat from Gaza, the Hezbollah rockets, which had been supplied by Iran and Syria, started raining down on northern Israel at a rate of over a hundred a day, killing and wounding scores of Israeli civilians in many cities including Safed, Nahariyah, Akko, and most notably Haifa, Israel's third largest city. Israel was forced to send thousands of troops back into Lebanon and Gaza to seek out and destroy the massive weaponry that had been amassed by Hezbollah in Lebanon and Hamas in Gaza. The nation of Israel, with the exception of most of Israel's Arab Muslim population, joined together in support of this necessary war for Israel's survival. Nonetheless, many questions need to be raised and lessons to be learned for the future. As we said, a full six years had passed since Israel's sudden flight from Lebanon. Did Ehud Barak and the rest of the Israeli leadership really expect the Hezbollah terrorists to sit politely with their hands folded for six years in a deep longing for peace? Did Ariel Sharon and his then deputy Ehud Olmert seriously think that the Hamas and Fatah terrorists would turn their swords into plowshares after Israel's retreat from Gaza? Did the American, European, and other leaders of the West sincerely believe that the Islamic terrorists would begin praying for the peace of Jerusalem, Uncle Sam, and the EU if we only "disengaged" from them by giving them control of more land from which to attack us? The lessons are clear, if we will only open our eyes, as we sit in our bomb shelters, as the missiles fall from the north and the south.

This brings us back to Sharon's grand statement of inclusion, which he declared over twenty years ago, at a time when I still respected him as a great Zionist visionary, for all the Jews in the world to join together in support of Israel. Frankly, I wish that was enough. I wish that all Jews would feel the pain of their brethren and cry out in support of God's Land, but after seeing the disappointing apathy of, and certainly, the lack of serious protest by most of the American Jewish leadership, as Israeli Jews were dragged from their homes in Gaza and northern Samaria, and after watching those secular Israeli leaders whose ignorance of Judaism is matched by their willingness, even eagerness, to give up the treasures of our Biblical heritage, I am convinced that just "the great Jewish project" is not enough. The time has come to welcome the support of the many millions of evangelical Christians who see God's Divine role in the return of Israel to Jerusalem, Shiloh, Hebron, Bethlehem, Beth El, and all the other holy Biblical sites. Yes, the time has come for everyone who believes that God has given Israel the responsibility of being "a kingdom of ministers and a holy nation" to stand up and be counted, not just for the State of Israel, but for the Biblical heartland of Israel. It is not enough for Christian believers from around the world to love Israel and pray for Israel and even to give monetary offerings to just any cause in Israel that comes to their attention. Support for Israel needs to be given in Biblically-consistent ways that support Biblical imperatives. **The retention of, and the building up of the Biblical heartland of Israel, in fulfillment of prophecy, is the greatest challenge in our times,** one that all people of faith should be actively supporting.

"Who is wise and will understand these things; who is understanding and will know them?" (Hosea 14:10)

As we discussed earlier, in June of 1967, God returned that embryo-shaped area, properly called Judea and Samaria, to Israel in six days, and then on the Sabbath day he rested. It is incomprehensible that He would perform such a miracle and then expect us to give it away to our enemies. To be a Zionist is to be a person of action. I believe that words of support and prayer for Samaria and Judea are not enough. One who loves Israel and its holy places needs to show his self-sacrifice for God's Land either with his body and blood as so many of us have, or with financial support for projects in the heartland, and with political support and activism on behalf of the heartland communities. It is the most powerful response to the Muslim threat against Western civilization, or as they say in Arabic, against "the Saturday people and the Sunday people." By helping the children in Shiloh and the other Biblical Lands not just to remain in their homes, but to thrive and develop and grow into adults who are strong believers in and are knowledgeable about their God-given inheritance, we are in essence declaring, "There is just one Father in Heaven, he gave His Land to His People and his name is not Allah!"

Every year, there is a well-publicized and well-attended gathering of political leaders held in the Israeli coastal city of Herzliya. Virtually all of the Israeli and American political leaders who spoke at the 2003 conference (which I remember well because it was held exactly two years after Ruby and I were wounded), advocated peace plans and road maps and various degrees of unilateral or agreed-upon Israeli withdrawals. With great intellectual pomp and fanfare, the recurring theme proposed by all of these supposedly brilliant strategists was Israeli retreat and relying on other countries, even hostile nations, to act on our behalf, as we withdraw from strategic assets. It was distressing that of all the "great thinkers" in Israel and from around the world who spoke at this conference, not one understood that Israel's peace strategy cannot be considered realistic if it is outside of the Biblical context.

However disappointing all of these speakers were, there was but one solitary light in the darkness of that conference. Pat Robertson, founder of the Christian Broadcasting Network and former presidential candidate, was invited to speak at the conference, presumably as a representative of evangelical Christians. However, despite the long list of Israeli speakers, he was, rather ironically, the only speaker who alluded to the importance of Israel's sacred mission as the guardians of the Land. Rather than discussing details of how much territory Israel should surrender to the Ishmaelite, he respectfully warned the Israeli leaders in attendance of the dangers of spurning their divine responsibility to protect God's Land.

"If God's chosen people turn over to Allah control of their most sacred sites – if they surrender to Muslim vandals the tombs of Rachel, of Joseph, of the Patriarchs, of the ancient Prophets – if they believe their claim to the Holy Land comes only from Lord Balfour of England and the ever fickle United Nations rather than the promises of Almighty God – then in that event, Islam will have won the battle."

(Pat Robertson, Herzliya Conference, 2003)

This statement by a well-known Christian leader undoubtedly raised the eyebrows of many Jews. It's a known fact that many American Jews and Israelis are wary of Christian support for Israel, especially if it is spoken in religious terms, but for me, it was a delightful breath of fresh air after hearing the depressing defeatist talk of my fellow citizens and seeing the lack of support from American Jews for the historic heartland of Israel.

If American Jewish leaders had the courage and/or understanding to speak with such moral clarity, I would be very happy. Unfortunately, it doesn't happen often enough. It would require a separate book to seriously analyze the reasons why, but I believe that it is partially a result of the religion of Secular Rationalism, which refuses to consider the Bible as anything more than an interesting collection of literary myths and legends. A second factor is undoubtedly the security of the material comforts in North America and the fear that standing up too strongly will "rock the boat" and awaken the genie of dual loyalty, as if American Jews don't have the right to be loyal American citizens and strong supporters of Israel at the same time. An additional complicating factor is that the American Jewish population is steadily shrinking in numbers, due to increasing intermarriage rates and a disproportionately low birthrate. In other words, their focus of concern is more and more pointing inwards.

As for my Israeli brethren, I only wish that the Religious Zionist public, who are among the most patriotic citizens in the State of Israel today, would be adequately represented as speakers at such conferences, to deliver an authentic Jewish perspective that is rarely heard in the left and secular-controlled Israeli media. The self-proclaimed democrats on the left side of the Israeli political spectrum are firm believers in freedom of speech and open political discourse, as long as the words being spoken fit the "liberal"-left agenda.

Many Jews don't quite know how to relate to the newfound but increasing evangelical supporters of Israel. For close to two thousand years, Jews were repeatedly subjected to forced conversions, aggressive proselytizing, and mass murder at the hands of the Christian (mostly Catholic) societies in which they dwelled. Suddenly, in recent years, we have the phenomenon of exuberant Christian supporters of Israel marching in the streets of Jerusalem on the Feast of Tabernacles (Sukkot) and at other times as well, waving little Israeli flags, and shouting, "We love you Israel. You are the apple of God's eye!" Many Jews are having difficulty adjusting to this new reality and are suspicious that the real intent of these visitors is to send out thousands of missionaries to attempt to convert us. It is extremely important for Christians to be sensitive to these concerns, because they didn't arise in a vacuum, as our earlier discussion about the Spanish Inquisition made clear. Yes, I know that proselytizing is central to Christianity, as Christians believe in their obligation to "spread the good news," but because of the historical sensitivities involved, sending missionaries out to convince the Jews that Jesus is the Messiah can only be destructive to the spirit of cooperation that we are trying to build. Israel's Covenant with God is to be respected and supported, as well as the integrity of our belief that the Messiah hasn't yet come, whether Christians agree with that belief or not. I have no doubt that when he does come, it will be clear to everyone who he is and whether he's been here before, but at this point, mutual tolerance of differences of opinion is crucial. Otherwise, the long-term theological disagreements will get in the way of the necessary cooperation. Besides, there are many millions of Muslims out there waiting to be convinced of the falsehood of Islam! That's where the missionaries' focus and energies should be placed, especially in these times. What greater contribution to world peace can there be than to persuade the Muslims to repent from the sword of Islam?

At the same time, it would be wise for Israeli Jews to overcome their misgivings, to get past the knee-jerk reactions, and to welcome the unconditional support of all those, Jew or Gentile, who recognize the importance and the spiritual dimension of Israel's revival and return to its God-given heartland, and ultimately to its Torah. This involves extending a hand in peace and friendship to an active segment of the American population that has substantial political influence, and should certainly be encouraged to use it on behalf of Israel. The Christian supporters of Israel have increasingly shown willingness, even eagerness, to identify with the People of Israel by supporting projects throughout Israel, including Judea and Samaria. In fact, the very first donations to the Shiloh Israel Children's Fund came from pro-Israel Christians, who instinctively understood, like many subsequent Jewish supporters, that when one donates to worthy causes in the heartland of Israel, he is responding to the enemies of the God of Abraham, Isaac, and Jacob, by asserting that God's Covenants with Israel are everlasting, and that the world will stand with the pioneers of Israel as they build for the future generations in the Biblical heartland. With the help of caring people from around the world, the tears and the traumas from the current terror wars and the foolish plans of the politicians will be permanently transformed, into the happy sounds of children learning, playing, and growing in their Land.

"...And the broad places of the city shall be full of girls and boys playing in the streets." (Zechariah 8:5)

"Restrain your voice from weeping and your eyes from tears...and your children will return to their borders" (Jeremiah 31:15-16)

Those who believe in the God of Israel know that supporting Israel in Biblically-consistent ways has its rewards, even though it is a value in and of itself, for those who help Israel are helping to fulfill God's purposes in this world. Those in the Gentile world who don't yet understand this would be wise to read chapter 12 in the Book of Genesis, in which the Lord made his eternal promise to the first Patriarch of Israel.

"God said to Abram, 'Go forth from your homeland, from your relatives, from your father's house, to the Land that I will show you; and I will make of you a great nation, and I will bless you, and make your name great, and you shall be a blessing. I will bless those that bless you, and him who curses you I will curse; and all the families of the earth shall be blessed through you." (Genesis 12:1-3)

Can it be stated any clearer? In other words, the path to God's blessings is through His Chosen People, and those who curse His Chosen People will be cursed. As stated earlier, the Covenants between God and Israel are everlasting, i.e., were never abrogated by either side, despite the ups and downs in the relationship. Therefore, anyone who denies this reality is denying the veracity of the Bible.

"And who is like your people Israel, one nation in the land, whom God went forth to redeem for Himself as a people." (I Chronicles 17:21)

Unfortunately, the People of Israel have not yet succeeded in their mission. The return of Israel to its ancestral, geographic, and spiritual heartland was clearly not a process that happened in order for Israel to turn around and give it all away to Israel's enemies. When Israel retreated from Gaza in the summer of 2005, it was in essence rejecting, at least for now, the Almighty's Plan of return to His Land and return to His Torah.

So then, with all the tragic events taking place in Israel today, we are forced to ask several serious questions, for if we don't confront these issues, we are in effect committing collective suicide and conceding defeat in the war on terrorism:

♦ Is Israel destined to always be a stiff-necked people, prone to self-destruction, and self-denial of its spiritual responsibility?

♦ Will the nations of the world continue to pretend that the Islamic threat is just from its "extremist fringe"?

♦ Will the heartland be surrendered to the forces of terrorism, and will Israel retreat to the coastline, before being driven into the sea?

♦ Is the miraculous rebirth of Israel to be undone?

The Redemption of Israel (and The World)

I have never claimed to be a prophet, even if I often stroll on the same hills on which Samuel the Prophet used to walk, but some things do seem obvious to me, as they were clear to our Sages many years ago. I suggest that we explore some of those concepts, which will give us a better perspective on the redemptive process and what lies ahead of us.

The redemption of Israel is referred to as a continuous process, analogous to the ascent to the strategic mountain range on which Shiloh is located. In order to ascend to the highest peaks, one must first raise oneself up to the lower peaks and even go down through the valleys along the way, before rising up again.

Through this analogy, one can begin to understand the difficult times that Israel has been suffering through. In addition to the terrorism and the expulsions of Jewish families from their homes, which have been inflicted disproportionately on the religious Zionist population, there has been a simultaneous increase in hedonism among the secular population, leading to more street crimes and sex crimes in the (mostly secular) cities of the coastal plain. A recent study (Jerusalem Post, May 8, 2006) reported that in 2005, there was a 30% rise in reports of group rape and incest. Along with all of these problems, we see the seemingly endless corruption of the political leadership, and we have even suffered from a lack of bold religious leadership to speak out about the solutions to these problems. All of the above represent what is known as, "The birth pangs of the Messiah."

"In the footsteps of the Messiah, insolence will increase and honor dwindle; the vine will yield its fruit abundantly, but the price will be

dear; the kingdom shall turn to heresy and there will be none to criticize; the meeting place of learning will be used for immorality...; the wisdom of the scribes will degenerate and the truth will be lacking...the face of the generation will be as the face of the dog..." (The Talmud, Sotah 49)

In these very same writings, we even see the results of the "Disengagement Plan", as well as the "Reengagement War", which devastated the Galilee region with the rockets of Hezbollah.

"In the footsteps of the Messiah, the Galilee will be destroyed." (The Talmud, Sotah 49)

"For the violence of Lebanon will cover you... for the violence of the land, of the city, and of all that dwell there." (Habakkuk 2:17)

"For Gaza will be deserted..." (Zephaniah 2:4)

The poetic Writings of the Prophets reveal the secrets of the Redemption of Israel, and consequently, of the world, but to understand these masterpieces, one frequently needs to look beyond the surface meaning of the text in order to grasp its deeper meanings. In referring to the Messianic era, the Prophet Isaiah (Isaiah 60) speaks of a time when the Holy Temple will be rebuilt, when all violence will cease in the Land, when Israel's sovereignty over the Land will be recognized by the world, and when the God of Israel will be recognized as the true God. Suddenly, at the very end of the chapter, there is a verse that seems a very strange way to sum up the process of Redemption.

"I am the Lord; in its time will I hurry it." (Isaiah 60:22)

In its time will I hurry it? It appears to be a contradictory statement! Either the Redemption will be hurried or it won't be! Well, before we accuse God of contradicting Himself or trying to confuse us for some reason, we would be well advised to refer to the writings of the Sages of Israel, who have certainly addressed this issue.

"If the Redemption has 'its time', a fixed and set time, then how will God hurry it? Either there is a set time or it is flexible." And the answer is: "If they (the Jews) merit it, I will hurry it. If they do not merit it, it will

come in its time." (The Talmud, Sanhedrin 98)

How simple, yet how frightening! The Sages of Israel have taught us that the promised Redemption will come in one of two ways. It will either come speedily and in a glorious way or it will come eventually (in its time), but with terrible suffering. And how does it come speedily (how will it be hurried)? When the People of Israel start to disengage from their secular ways, and start to walk in the ways of their God. Even in Western society, it's no secret that there has been a moral struggle for several decades between the forces of moral relativism, who say that truth is relative, and those who believe that there is such a thing as absolute truth and morality, based on God's Biblical guidelines for life.

"For moral absolutes, we have substituted moral ambiguity. We now communicate with everyone and say absolutely nothing...Our society finds truth a medicine too strong to digest undiluted...What Moses brought down from Mount Sinai were not the Ten Suggestions. They are commandments. Are, not were. The sheer brilliance of the Ten Commandments is that they codify in a handful of words acceptable human behavior, not just for then or now, but for all time."
(TV News personality Ted Koppel,
Commencement Address at Duke University, May 10, 1987)

In Israel, the struggle between moral relativism and the truth of Torah is that much more intense. Though the basic principle of the societal conflict is similar to that in Western society, this moral struggle in Israel has enormous ramifications for the world. As God's chosen people, every Jew, by choosing the path of Torah to whatever extent, can help to create a better world. Let me be clear about this, for the sake of any secular Jews who are reading this. As one who came from a secular lifestyle (see Chapter One), I know that gradual change is easier and more stable than abrupt changes in one's lifestyle, but it's still unsettling, because we like to stick with what feels comfortable. Just go to any college classroom and you will see that the students sit in the same seats at every lesson, even though there are no assigned seats, and certainly no one would get punished for choosing a different seat. We like to stick with what's comfortable, even in such mundane matters. But one who has experienced miracles cannot look the other way and pretend that they don't occur. While I firmly believe that there is free choice in this world, and that one needs to decide for him or herself, the People of Israel that has experienced so many miracles not just since the rise of the State of Israel, but throughout its history, cannot afford to look the other way. So the first step is to begin to walk in the direction of connecting to Jewish heritage, in whatever way it feels comfortable. It is essentially a strategic decision to choose life. Once that choice is made, the extent and the pace of any process depends on the individual. But to remain spiritually stagnant and ignorant of one's heritage is never a good choice. Unfortunately, much of Israel is moving in the opposite direction, running after the foreign gods of rampant materialism and self-destructive hedonism, some even referring to the stock market as "the new Zionism" and the drug culture as "the new-age spirituality"!

Is this to become a continuous downward spiral for Israel and the world, contrary to our understanding of the process of redemption? Could it perhaps result in a third exile from the Land of Israel? Will the Israelis continue to ignore their great inheritance and their role as spiritual leaders, essentially spitting in the "face" of the Lord who gave it to them? How will the various Christian denominations relate to Israel in these tumultuous yet critical times that we are living through? And what is the role of the re-established community of Shiloh in all of this?

Chapter Ten

To The Future

"Because they hated knowledge and did not choose fear of the Lord, they refused my counsel, they despised all my reproof; and therefore they shall eat of the fruits of their own path, and be filled with their own devices."   *(Proverbs 1:29-31)*

As discussed earlier, former Prime Minister Ariel Sharon was the architect, or at least the aggressive and enthusiastic implementer, of the so-called Disengagement Plan of 2005, in which thousands of Jews were expelled from their homes, lost their jobs, and had their beautiful communities destroyed. Exactly one day before Sharon had a massive stroke and went into a lengthy coma, police investigators claimed to have found evidence of a three million dollar bribe that Mr. Sharon allegedly had received from one of the major international investors in the Palestinian Authority's Jericho Casino (Jerusalem Post, January 3, 2006).

> "I guarantee that any man who does not have the fear of God will be a corrupt ruler; he will be crooked and dishonest. No man can exercise leadership over others unless he is conscious that he, himself, is ruled. No man can rule who is not ruled himself."
>
> *(Pastor Chuck Smith, Living Water: P.240)*

In the period leading up to the Disengagement, there had been scathing reports of alleged shady dealings (see the book, *Boomerang*, Shelach and Drucker, 2005), which helped to explain Sharon's abrupt change from active supporter of settlement to active destroyer. Perhaps we will never know the full truth, and there certainly are those who still have an interest in burying the allegations, but it appears to me, and to many others, that personal corruption may have been a major motivating factor in the tragic decisions of Israel's leaders to withdraw from Gush Katif and the other beautiful communities that were destroyed.

"Only those with a pure soul, following a pristine path according to God's Torah, can achieve heartfelt empathy for the communal suffering."
(Rabbi A.Y. Kook, Lights of Repentance, 13:4)

"Through justice a king establishes a land, but a man of graft tears it down." *(Proverbs 29:4)*

This is the sad reality that we are living with today as the Land is being torn apart in front of our eyes. On the White House lawn in 1993, the Israeli government agreed, in exchange for empty promises, to negotiate the surrender of its ancestral homeland with the terrorists of the PLO, the organizational forerunner of the Palestinian Authority. Just thirteen years and thousands of innocent Israeli civilian deaths later, nothing has been learned, as a morally corrupt and unrestrained Israeli government considers, despite all the talk to the contrary, doing the same with the Hamas, the extreme Islamic terror group that is the equivalent of Al Qaeda, but that was democratically elected in 2006 to be the dominant force in the Palestinian Authority. Then Israeli Defense Minister Shaul Mofaz made those intentions clear (Jerusalem Post, January 6, 2006), when he stated that Israel would negotiate with Hamas if it "ceased acts of terror" and changed its charter calling for Israel's destruction. Does that mean that if they take a break, with perhaps a long-term truce, in order to re-arm and concentrate on increasing the range of their Kassam and/ or Katyusha rockets so that they can reach metropolitan Tel Aviv, we will then negotiate with them the extent of our surrender? Will we negotiate with them if they let other terror groups carry out the attacks, but don't actually do it themselves? Deputy Prime Minister Shimon Peres (Israel National News, April 5, 2006) went a step further, declaring that in order to reach "peace," Israel should negotiate with anyone, including Hamas.

I once heard a wise man say that it's smarter to learn from the mistakes of others rather than from your own, but you should also learn from your own mistakes. However, both Israel and the Western world seem to be doing neither. In short, we all still seem willing to accept more promises and perhaps more pieces of worthless paper agreements in exchange for the most tangible of Israel's assets, its land and water supplies, and of course the historic, Biblical sites, precious to all believers in the God of Abraham, Isaac, and Jacob. Haven't we been in this movie before? Have we learned nothing from the past thirteen years of trying to turn the Fatah terrorists into peace partners? Why do we think that it will be different with Hamas? If anything, it will be far worse. Did we not see the Kassam rockets flying daily over the Gaza "security" fence in the south of the country, on the innocent civilians in the cities of Sderot and Ashkelon? Do we not see the hundreds of Hezbollah Katyushas falling on cities in the north, including Haifa, the third largest city in Israel?

All this has happened AFTER the unilateral retreat from Gaza, which post-dated by five years the unilateral retreat from Lebanon. The Muslim terrorists rightly interpret such withdrawals as acts of weakness and fear. Former Prime Ministers Ehud Barak and Ariel Sharon, as well as Sharon's former sidekick and successor in the new Kadima Party, Ehud Olmert, had promised improved security as a result of the withdrawals! Instead, in one short year, we reached a point where senior IDF officers (Jerusalem Post, March 8, 2006) began expressing their helplessness in preventing those same Kassam rocket attacks being launched daily over the preventative Gaza security fence in the south. Then in July of 2006 came the "surprising" flood of Hezbollah rocket attacks over the Lebanon security fence in the north onto Israeli cities, which Israel was forced to respond to by returning to Lebanon in addition to Gaza with air attacks and ground troops. Hundreds of Israelis were killed or wounded in a month of fighting. After a month of indecisive leadership during the war, Prime Minister Olmert hastily agreed to a U.N. ceasefire plan through which Hezbollah would keep its weapons. Is this the reason why several thousands of Israel's children had to spend a month in bomb shelters? What do we have to show for our losses? Furthermore, why was the Hezbollah military buildup ignored for six years?

As for the rocket attacks in the south, what did we gain from the expulsion of several thousands of children, many of whom were terror victims, from their homes, and throwing their parents into a state of chronic unemployment? The vibrant yeshivas (religious seminaries), schools, and synagogues of the beautiful Jewish communities

in Gaza were ransacked, set on fire, and destroyed by the "peace partners" of the Palestinian Authority. Can our enemies take seriously
our repeated empty threats to "hit back hard", when we callously
disregarded the pain of our dedicated civilian brethren on the front
lines?

*"Those who are kind to those who are cruel will ultimately be cruel
to those who are kind." (Midrash Yalkut Shimoni)*

Do we really believe that ignoring the suffering of Israeli civilians, while retreating from our enemies will solve our problems? Most
importantly, will the lessons from the rocket attacks be learned by
Israel and the free world?

"We left Lebanon to the last centimeter, and they are firing. We left Gaza to the last centimeter, and they are firing. What
we have learned is that if they lay down their arms there will be
peace, but if we lay down our arms, they will slaughter us."
*(Former Prime Minister Binyamin Netanyahu,
Knesset Speech, August 14, 2006)*

"Those who cannot learn from history are doomed to
repeat it."
(George Santayana, The Life of Reason, Volume One, 1905)

"It's a great mistake to learn from history. There is nothing to learn from history."
(Oslo Accords Architect Shimon Peres, Maariv, May 23, 1996)

Nothing to learn from history? What other people have a greater
need to learn from history than the People of Israel? The nation that
received the Torah on Mount Sinai has nothing to learn from history?
The nation that lived through almost 2,000 years of persecution has
nothing to learn from history? What about the United States and the
rest of the free world? With its firm principles of freedom and democracy and its pride in its Biblical foundations, doesn't the United
States have what to learn from history?

Nonetheless, this failure to learn from history has been evident
in all of the "road maps" supported by the U.S. and Europe, but is
especially glaring in current Prime Minister Ehud Olmert's "Conver-

gence or Realignment Plan" (Yediot Acharonot, March 5, 2006) intended to destroy many more of Israel's finest and most historic, not
to mention strategic communities, including Shiloh! This had been
whispered about for some time, but not declared publicly, presumably so as not to disturb the Kadima Party's 2006 election campaign.
The status quo was broken when a high-ranking candidate in Olmert's
Kadima revealed his boss's intentions on all the front pages. On the
very next day, evidence surfaced (Jerusalem Post, March 6, 2006), about
alleged corruption scandals surrounding the Kadima Party, headed
by, you guessed it, Ehud Olmert, Ariel Sharon's successor. The corruption scandal allegations against Ariel Sharon and his sons, followed
by the various allegations against Ehud Olmert do not surprise me.
When one takes heartless actions that are immoral, such as expelling
thousands of Jewish children from their homes in the Land of Israel,
and seeks to do it again in the future on a much larger scale against
those living in the Biblical heartland, it has to stem from the most
impure motives. Yet much of the Israeli public seemed to ignore the
investigations of alleged corruption, and appeared if not to whole-
heartedly support, at least to accept the proposed withdrawals and
expulsions.

On March 28, 2006, the Israeli electorate voted in large numbers
for Olmert's Kadima Party. While they received far less votes than the
pollsters had predicted, second place was taken by the equally pro-
withdrawal Labor Party. While some may convincingly argue that the
election results were based more on social issues than on Olmert's
new expulsion plan, the fact is that the public was willing, at least for
a while, to ignore his withdrawal plans. Since then, with the outbreak
of the "Reengagement War" in Israel and in Lebanon, Israeli public
opinion shifted to the extent that in July of 2006, barely 28% was in
support of the idea of further retreats (Poll: July 17-18, Maagar Mochot
Survey Institute). Nonetheless, and even while the rockets were falling, and while Israeli children were forced to sit for weeks in bomb
shelters, Prime Minister Olmert, assisted by his enthusiastic deputy
Tzippi Livni, continued promoting his plan, which is essentially a strategy of continuing the pattern of retreat under enemy attack, by surrendering the heartland of Israel to the Islamic terrorists.

"The (extensive) training in preparation for the Disengagement, and the enthusiasm of its initiator, forced our mili-

tary to stop preparing for war... It is almost certain that our losing the war was related to this."
(Israeli General Yiftach Ron-Tal, Maariv October 4, 2006)

Prime Minister Ehud Olmert was ultimately forced to resign in the fall of 2008 under the threat of indictment for a long list of corruption charges. Nonetheless, neither he nor his coterie of followers seemed to have learned the lesson that some of his top commanders have learned, and after the poor handling of the conflict with Hezbollah, they spent the next two years pushing the same foolish "peace" plans.

Olmert and Livni have pushed forward such plans by stressing the demographic factor, that the Arabs greatly outnumber the Jews in Judea and Samaria (the West Bank). This argument ignores both the very high birthrates of the Jewish residents of Judea and Samaria and the rising emigration of the Arabs from those areas. Furthermore, the media rarely notes that the reports of massive Muslim Arab population growth have been deliberately falsified (see Israel National News: September 25, 2008) to serve Muslim/Arab interests. We ignore these two simultaneous trends at our own peril. In fact, one of the biggest problems in Shiloh is that there aren't enough homes for all of the young couples and families who want to live there. Conversely, there has been a steady flow of emigration of well-to-do Arabs from the neighboring Arab village of Turmus Aya to North and Central America (see New York Times: July 29, 2002).

The real demographic problem for Israel is in the Galilee, which already has an Arab majority, as well as in medium-sized cities with large and growing Arab minorities, such as Lod and Ramle in central Israel, adjacent to Ben-Gurion International Airport. That coupled with secular Jewish birthrates barely at replacement level, and the rising secular Jewish **emigration** from Israel, and we can see that indeed the demographic dilemma is not in Shiloh, with its high birthrates, or in the rest of the Biblical heartland of Judea and Samaria with its high Jewish birthrates of 4.4 children per family (Israel National News, Nov. 26, 2006), but rather in pre-1967 Israel. As one distressed secular Israeli grandmother told me recently on a plane ride to the United States to visit her children and grandchildren, "Almost every family living in the greater Tel Aviv area has a son or a daughter that has left Israel to live in the United States or Europe."

Even Olmert has two adult sons who have chosen to live their lives abroad. On the other hand, it is almost unheard of for a child of Shiloh, Beth El, or Hebron to permanently leave the country. So where is the real demographic problem?

Unfortunately, such reasoned debate carries little weight with too many of the secular Israelis who are emotionally searching for a panacea, rather than a realistic solution. This Israeli yearning for any quick answer, in the hopes that it may bring the (temporary) approval of the great American surrogate parent (the President), which hopefully will enable us to "Don't worry, be happy", as the popular Israeli expression goes, is symptomatic of a teenage-like impetuousness and lack of maturity in the ways of the world. The teenager who wants what he wants when he wants it, has always frustrated real-life parents, who see their almost physically mature teenagers often acting like young children. I have no doubt that God sees his children Israel in the same light. On one hand, Israel wants (the promise of) peace now, immediately, and seems to have almost no red lines as to what it is willing to give away in exchange for this pipe dream. Just as the teenager often doesn't think about the future ramifications of his actions, and therefore, acts impetuously, so too with Israel today.

One of the more astute political analysts in Israel today is a columnist named Sarah Honig. In a recent column (Jerusalem Post, March 31, 2006), she quotes the late Natan Alterman, one of the most renowned Zionist poets both before and after the rise of the State. After his death in 1970, several previously unpublished poems were discovered. In one of these, entitled "Then Satan Said", he addressed the malaise of an Israeli population that, even then, several years after the Six-Day War, was losing a basic belief in its right to the Land:

"…Satan then said:
How do I overcome this besieged one?
He has courage and talent
And implements of war
And resourcefulness.
…only this shall I do,
I'll dull his mind
And cause him to forget
The justice of his cause."

(Natan Alterman)

The seeming eagerness to part with the ancestral places appears to contradict the issue-based surveys, which repeatedly say that the majority of Israelis believe that the Oslo Accords were a mistake. So what has changed? In the Oslo Accords, Israel received promises of peace from the Palestinian Authority, but they weren't honored. The Olmertian unilateral approach says that if the other side (the Hamas-led P.A.) doesn't agree to more such agreements, we'll teach them a lesson that they'll never forget by withdrawing without getting anything in return!

Such logic from the Prime Minister of Israel reminds me of my days growing up in Brooklyn. If a bully threatened you demanding to take your money, what would be the most sensible response? Would you tell him that if he doesn't leave you alone, you'll get really tough with him by giving him your money? Such is the logic of Israel's current leadership. What person who believes deeply in his country also believes that it is better to **unilaterally** give away tangible assets such as land, and historic, strategic, and sacred places, **receiving nothing in return?**

"There are slaves with free spirits; there are free men with the spirit of slaves."
(Rabbi A.Y. Kook: Articles, P.157)

Just as a physically mature, but emotionally immature adolescent wants instant gratification for his adult desires, and he often doesn't have the patience to see the full picture, so too, Israel, in its second adolescent period still lacks the maturity to have patience, yet to stand firm, **and to see that the full picture can only be understood according to God's plan.**

"Return, O wayward children – the word of the Lord – for I shall be your master." *(Jeremiah 3:14)*

In Chapter Three, we discussed the period of 369 years when the Tabernacle stood in Shiloh as the capital and center for the Children of Israel. We referred to this as Israel's first adolescent period, a period of time during which Samuel the Prophet grew up in Shiloh in the Lord's service, but the people as a whole lacked the maturity, unity, and independence of a post-adolescent nation. The Land had been conquered to some extent, but there were still many pockets of enemy resistance that were being ignored by Israel rather than being confronted. Joshua's urging the people to go out and take the initiative (Joshua 18:3) rather than waiting for their Daddy (God) to do it all for them, epitomized a nation still struggling with its own maturity issues. The manifest dependence exhibited by bringing the Holy Ark itself to the battlefield as a sort of panacea to fight Israel's battles (The Battle of Even-HaEzer), as opposed to standing on their own two feet and fighting back (on their own) with the faith that the Almighty would support their valiant military struggles, led to the defeat, the taking of the Ark of the Covenant, and eventually to the destruction of Shiloh.

We are apparently reliving that adolescent period in our times, that period of semi-sovereignty and physical maturity, combined with a psychological immaturity and a serious lack of self-confidence and genuine national pride that comes from within (as opposed to false Israeli macho). However, the current second adolescence in Shiloh does not have to end destructively, as did the first. We have come home to Shiloh, to our ancient capital. If we act properly in fulfilling God's plan, we can be the catalyst for the ascent to true sovereignty and unity and the building of the Third Temple in Jerusalem.

"The scepter shall not depart from Judah, nor a scholar from among his descendants, until Shiloh comes, and his shall be an assemblage of nations." (Genesis 49:10)

The Biblical commentators have much to say about this verse. The imperative to Israel not to remove the scepter, or the kingship of Israel, from the tribe of Judah was actually breached, not by Israel, but by the invading armies of Nebuchadnezzar, when Jerusalem, including the first Holy Temple of Israel, was destroyed. From then on, there was no king from the tribe of Judah. But what about those confusing, yet dramatic words, "...until Shiloh comes"? We all know, especially those who are reading this book, that Shiloh is an important place in the Land of Israel. Yes, it's a very significant city in Israel's history, the place where Joshua established the first permanent capital of Israel, where Hannah prayed for a son, where her son Samuel the Prophet grew up into prophecy. Shiloh is also central in the return of the People of Israel to its Biblical heartland, and geographically stands in the way of the building of a terrorist Hamas state in the heartland of Israel.

All of this is true, but it still doesn't seem to explain the expression, "until Shiloh comes." How can a place be referred to as a person? Most of the Biblical commentators are in agreement that the word "Shiloh" is synonymous with the Messiah, that the word "Shiloh" actually means "Messiah." So the obvious question that needs to be asked is, "What is the reason why this important place in Israel's history, and present, was chosen to be synonymous with the most important person in Israel's future (and the future of the entire world)? Since we believe that there are no coincidences in the Torah and every Hebrew letter has numerical value, the Lubavitcher Rebbe points out an interesting Kabbalistic connection (not to confuse this genuine source of Torah wisdom with its confused and out-of-context commercialization by several Hollywood celebrities) between the most important person in Israel's past, and Israel's Messiah, as represented by Shiloh:

"The Hebrew words *yavo Shiloh* (until Shiloh comes) are the numerical value of Mashiach (Messiah), and Shiloh is the numerical value of Moshe (Moses)."

> *(Rabbi Menachem Mendel Schneerson:*
> *quoted from Highlights of Moshiach,*
> *by Rabbi Abraham Stone, 1991)*

Clearly, Shiloh has a crucial role to play in the Messianic Process, but what is that role? From my research into this question, I believe that the answer can be found by looking at two significant quotes relating to Shiloh and its role in Israel's history and the redemptive process. We repeat the words that Joshua spoke to the Children of Israel in Shiloh:

"How long will you wait, to come and take possession of the land that the Lord, God of your fathers has given you?" (Joshua 18:3)

This imperative to take control of the Land is central in the redemptive process. The fact that these words were delivered by Joshua in Shiloh seems to indicate the centrality of Shiloh in that process. This, together with the labeling of Shiloh as being synonymous with

Messiah, appears to strengthen the supposition that the restoration and development of Shiloh is a crucial factor in the redemptive process through which Israel will reach its full spiritual maturity.

"Then I will sprinkle clean water upon you, and you shall be clean: from all your uncleanness and from all your idols, will I cleanse you. A new heart also will I give you, and a new spirit will I put within you...I will put my spirit within you and cause you to follow my statutes, and you shall keep my judgments and do them. And you shall dwell in the land that I gave to your fathers; and you shall be my people, and I will be your God." (Ezekiel 36:25-28)

This spiritual awakening is evident in the Shiloh bloc of communities. In fact, the spelling of the name Shiloh, itself denotes a

The Tabernacle Synagogue in Shiloh: *Architecturally based on the Tabernacle that once stood in Shiloh, this place of worship symbolizes Israel's return to its heartland and to its roots.*

spiritual revival, while its often incorrect English transliteration (perhaps inadvertently) represents the spiritual struggle. It's interesting to note that most of the road signs in modern secular Israel, and many of the maps, write Shiloh in English as "Shilo", without the letter "h" at the end. The word Shiloh without the "h" (in Hebrew) simply means "calm" or "tranquility." The letter "h" corresponds with the Hebrew letter "hey", which denotes the presence of God. For example, the first Hebrews, Abram and Sarai, (see Book of Genesis) had the letter "hey" or "h", added to their names, partially in recognition of their new level of spiritual maturation. Spelling Shiloh without its "h" symbolically represents the attempts of the anti-religious forces to push back the spiritual advances that we have made here in the Biblical heartland. But the spiritual presence in Shiloh is getting stronger, as the nucleus for the future spiritual strength of Israel grows upward and outward onto its hills and into its valleys.

There is a relevant discussion in the Talmud that provides strong backing to the centrality of Shiloh in Israel's spiritual awakening and maturation. This discussion blends together the concepts of Shiloh both as the resting place (or place of tranquility) and as the focus of Israel's spiritual awakening, or maturation:

"To the resting place, and to the inheritance. To the resting place – this is Shiloh. The inheritance – this is Jerusalem." (Zevachim 119A)

There is a sequence of events in the redemptive process. Just as Jerusalem could not be established and the Holy Temple built there, representing the united kingdom of Israel, until Shiloh had its period both as the site of Israel's maturation process, and the maturation process of the young prophet Samuel, who was destined to appoint King David to the throne; so too, we appear to be in a similar sequence of events today. The reborn Shiloh of today is a center of dedication to the Land of Israel and its Torah, and has an important role to play as a leader of the redemptive process for Israel and ultimately for all mankind. The beautiful synagogue in Shiloh, built as a replica of the Tabernacle, is a powerful symbol of Israel's return to its heartland. The (as yet unfinished) study hall building of the Shiloh Yeshiva (which combines army service with high-level religious studies) has 13 domes, representing the gematria, or numerical expression, of the Hebrew word, *Echad*, or "One," symbolizing the oneness

A Future Beacon of Light and Unity: *The Shiloh Yeshiva building represents a vision of faith in Israel's future as a spiritual light unto the nations.*

of God and the unity of His purpose, and I might add, the eventual unity of all the nations of the world who will proclaim and praise His holy name.

> *"God will be King over all the land; on that day the Lord will be One and His Name will be One." (Zechariah 14:9)*

In other words, on that day, there will be no confusion or disagreement between Jews and Christians about "the Messiah question" or any other questions of theology. All of the theological disagreements that have tragically been the catalyst, even the excuse, for so much Jewish pain and bloodshed in the past will remain in the past. There will be unprecedented unity among the peoples of the world in the desire to praise God in the proper way, which will be clear to all of us on that day. There will be no disagreements over who is the Messiah, who will be saved, or whose theology is correct. Obviously, I am referring to the ongoing theological differences between Jews and Christians, but we are not the only peoples in this world. Yes, perhaps even the Muslims will have their eyes opened and will abandon the violent, destructive falsehood that is called Islam.

> *"Many peoples will go and say, 'Come, let us go up to God's Mountain, to the Temple of the God of Jacob (Israel), and He will teach us of*

His ways and we will walk in His paths. For from Zion will go forth the Torah, and the word of the Lord from Jerusalem. He will judge among the nations, and will settle the arguments of many peoples. They shall beat their swords into plowshares and their spears into pruning hooks; nations will not lift sword against nation and they will no longer study warfare." (Isaiah 2:3-4)

Therefore, the closed-mindedness among some Jews and some Christians, that prevents good people from working together on the many issues that unite us is, in my opinion, a blatant rejection of the prophetic vision that should be impelling all believers in the true God and His Torah to try to make that vision of cooperation a reality in our times.

How Do We Get To That Stage?

"Unto your seed have I given this Land from the river of Egypt until the great river, the River Euphrates" (Genesis 15:18)

"Behold, I have taught you statutes and judgments, even as the Lord, my God, commanded me, that you shall do so in the Land to which you come, to possess it." (Deuteronomy 4:5)

"I will bless those who bless you, and him who curses you I will curse; and all the families of the earth shall bless themselves through you." (Genesis 12:3)

These three Biblical quotes, when read together, captivate the essence of the struggle for the Land of Israel in our times, for they each correspond to fundamental imperatives for all the peoples of the world in these tumultuous times:

♦ The clear instruction to Israel and the world regarding the deed to the entire Land of Israel.

♦ The responsibility of the People of Israel to follow God's commandments for them, and to do so in the Land of Israel.

♦ The rewards for those righteous Gentiles who bless (assist) Israel in a way that is consistent with, and supportive of, imperatives 1 and 2.

These are frustrating, yet exciting times we are living in. There are those who find the challenges overwhelming and emphasize the half-empty cup rather than the half-full cup. Meir Stein, one of the founding fathers of the re-established Shiloh community, recently had a conversation with a relatively new home owner in another community in Samaria, who happened to be a new immigrant from France. This was shortly after one of the worst waves of terror, combined with a period of Israeli government weakness towards the Arabs and hostility towards the pioneers in the heartland. The man remarked," I won't do any renovations on my house with such uncertainty in the air. Any day now, they may try to give my house away!" The seasoned veteran from Shiloh responded calmly with the smile of one who's heard such comments before, "We have gone through so many ups and downs, and so many periods when things looked bad, but because we didn't let the tough times depress our spirit, we have weathered the storm and come out of it even stronger. If we had all stayed in the city and not insisted on settling the heartland, we would have lost everything by now. Furthermore, we raised a generation of young people with a natural strength and idealism, a generation that is prepared to fight for this Land with the complete faith that it is our God-given inheritance."

It is perhaps a frightening time of world conflict for many, but I also see it as a time of great clarification that we are living through. As discussed earlier, for many years, the Arabs of the Land of Israel spoke with two voices. The Palestinian Authority would speak in English to the world, proclaiming their desire for peace, while in Arabic they would declare their unswerving commitment to "the armed struggle" until the "liberation" of Jerusalem, Haifa, and Jaffa. The election of the Hamas terror organization has removed the mask that once covered the face of the English-speaking version of the Palestinian Authority. The Hamas, at least as of yet, refuses to shield its core beliefs from the public view. This clarification of views is a healthy process that may actually succeed in awakening the sleeping People of Israel and the slumbering nations of the world.

In addition, we may soon see a clarification of views among the People of Israel. Much has been written in the media about "the illegal hilltop outposts." These hilltops are actually burgeoning communities, consisting of young, idealistic families, usually living in what are known as "caravans", low-frills non-mobile trailer homes. These hilltops often become thriving communities in their own right, or become satellite neighborhoods of the more established towns. As a former mayor of Shiloh, I can tell you that most of these hilltop communities are situated within the municipal boundaries of the larger, more established towns, such Shiloh, Kedumim, or Beth El. Several of the hilltop communities have land claim complications or are in the midst of impending sales of land, which can certainly be resolved peacefully by people of good will. Furthermore, most Arabs are afraid to sell their own privately owned land, for fear that they will be murdered by their own brethren.

In February of 2006, then Acting Prime Minister Ehud Olmert (Yes, the same man who had proclaimed that we are tired of fighting our enemies!) ordered thousands of police to the hilltop community of Amona, near the town of Ofra, about a ten minute drive south of Shiloh, to destroy nine homes in which young families were living. The area was declared a closed military zone, thereby making any protest of the police action illegal. Nonetheless, hundreds of mostly young people came out to protest the destruction, many sitting down in and around the nine homes, in the spirit of passive, non-violent sit-down protest. The police on horseback trampled into the crowd, beating the young protesters on the heads with clubs and there was great bloodshed, with at least 200 protesters and police hospitalized. Even several Knesset members, including Benny Elon, Aryeh Eldad, and Effie Eitam, who had come to Amona to show their support for peaceful protest, were attacked and injured by the police, as well.

Coming on the heels of the Hamas election victory, which one might have expected to unify Israel, the scenes of internal violence shocked Israel, Jews, and lovers of Israel around the world. An Israeli commission of inquiry was established by the Knesset, despite the opposition of the Olmert Administration, to investigate the causes of those horrible events. After the 2006 elections in Israel, the Olmert Administration had the responsibility to continue or discontinue the mandate of this commission to investigate the events in Amona. Unfortunately, the right decision wasn't made, and those who were responsible most likely will not be forced to take responsibility, even if and especially if the orders to brutally attack were given from the political echelon.

After these recent internal struggles in Israel, many people have wondered why these most vehement protestors were the youth, who seemed to have no fear of the police brutality that they had heard was being ordered from above, and that they eventually encountered as the police-driven horses plowed over the peaceful protesters. Let it be clearly stated, the young people who were born in and grew up in the holiness of the Biblical heartland are integrally entwined with it, but many have been scarred by the battles to date. After the traumas of Gaza and Amona, they aren't willing to happily roll over and play dead, peacefully surrendering their homes to the Arabs' terrorist gangs that would eventually become the unworthy recipients of this gift from the foolish political leaders of secular Israel.

"Out of the mouths of babes and sucklings, You have established strength..." (Psalms 8:3)

Despite this painful internecine conflict, I believe that these events and any future (hopefully peaceful) conflict in the struggle for the Land of Israel, may lead to a clarification of views within Israel. There is a very popular Israeli singer named Yehoram Gaon, who also hosts a weekly radio show. Certainly not known for conservative or even right-of-center political views, he had quite a bit to say about the painful conflict in Amona, and what it means for the future of Zionism.

Let's read several of the comments he made on his radio show after the events in Amona:

"...it appears that the youth no longer have leaders other than this land. The land is leading and directing and forcing its will, and sending them to fight for it, and they agree to do so – like a lover for his loved one, with great truth and without compromise. Zionism '06."

"I know it's not popular today to say nice things about the settlers. All my colleagues in radio and television are very, very angry at them – but what to do? Only one who fights for his land, cities, and fields, and for every caravan and every clod of earth, acquires it, by virtue of his love and dedication."

"...Hand on heart: How many of us would leave our warm house, our dreams of getting rich, our cafes and nightclubs...to be with the Land of Israel, that it should not remain alone? How many of us, out of our own free will, would spend time on a barren, wind-swept hill in a caravan?" *(Yehoram Gaon, Israel Radio's Reshet Bet, February 3, 2006)*

Yehoram Gaon described the dedication to, and willingness to sacrifice for the Land of Israel as Zionism '06. Actually, sacrificing for the Land of Israel should be one of those "core curriculum" required college courses, which we could perhaps call Zionism 101. Either way, there is no question that this is the path to the redemption of the Land of Israel. When combined with our commitment to the individual and societal guidelines in God's Torah, we have the winning recipe. This dedication to the Land of Israel and God's Torah is evident in the rapidly rising number (now approximately 50%) of religious students in the army's officer training course. Those are the young people who best understand that God's Land is worth fighting for, and who are destined to be the future leadership of this nation. Could it be that this is the worst nightmare of many of the secular elites who rule Israel? Could this be the real reason why Olmert seems obsessed with retreating from the Biblical heartland? Perhaps it is or perhaps it isn't, but I have no doubt that the willingness to suffer and sacrifice for the Land and Torah of Israel is what will save this country, and thus save the entire world from the forces of Islam that threaten to destroy all of us.

That is the role of the People of Israel, in our times especially. But what about the righteous Gentile supporters of Israel, specifically those who strive to keep the basic moral laws incumbent upon all people? These noble individuals have a crucial supporting role to play in the redemptive process, especially in these fateful times, when the spokesmen for immorality are trying to take over Western society from within, and when the evil forces of Islam are seeking to violently take over the free world in any way possible. The admirable and valiant efforts to restore family values in the Western World and the unflinching support of many Christians for Israel, including the Biblical heartland, are worthy of great praise. But as it says in Genesis 12, those who don't bless Israel will be cursed.

"For behold, in those days and at that time, when I will bring back the captivity of Judah and Jerusalem, I will gather all of the nations and

bring them down to the Valley of Jehoshaphat and I will contend with them there concerning My people and my possession Israel, that they dispersed among the nations, and they divided up My land..." (Joel 4:1-2)

Yes, our Father in Heaven will bring forth a day of reckoning, and those Gentiles who did not support the Biblical heartland will be "contended with", as the Prophet said. Conversely, those who help in the struggle for the Land will be blessed! Working concurrently and in cooperation, with complete faith that our actions will be supported from above, I have no doubt that we can overcome the forces of terrorism and destruction, both in Israel and in the entire world.

The prophet Jeremiah, at the time of the siege on Jerusalem, shortly before the destruction of the First Temple, was told by God to go out and buy a field (Jeremiah 32:24-25). The question might be asked, "What kind of crazy time is that to invest in Israeli real estate?" The great Zionist visionary, Rabbi Tzvi Yehuda Kook gives the answer to this seemingly simple question:

"Prophecy which was not needed for future generations was recorded, and prophecy not needed for the generations to come was not recorded (=Megilla 14A). There is prophecy which was spoken to a generation for problems specific to it (specific to that generation), yet its value (the value of the prophecy) extends to all times." (Torat Eretz Yisrael, p.187) In other words, the pressure of the many misguided leaders in America and Europe, and the defeatism of the many Israeli leaders of little faith, these are not what should guide us; rather we should be led by the Divine instructions given to us through the ages, which are still applicable in our times, more than ever. Whatever the results will be, we will at the very least know that we did the right thing, by following the right guidelines.

"The Lord shall reign forever and ever, your God of Zion; from generation to generation. Halleluyah!" (Psalms 146:10)

Those were the words of King David, the great poet and warrior, who sat on the throne in Jerusalem with the Torah at his side. There was never any doubt that God's covenant with Israel was everlasting and that Zion, meaning the Land of Israel, was and always would be, the center of His presence. From Zion, the word of the Lord would gradually spread out to the nations, until there would be no more doubts as to His omnipotence.

When Joshua Bin Nun, the great conqueror of the Land, who would eventually lead the Children of Israel to their resting place in Shiloh, took over for Moses, God gave him clear instructions as to our destiny in the Land of Israel. He listened very carefully to these words, and it is incumbent on all of us, as well, to remember and to adhere to them in our times, for it is clear that if we do, the blessings will be great for all of us.

"Every place upon which the sole of your foot will tread I have given to you, as I spoke to Moses." (Joshua 1:3)

"This Book of the Torah shall not depart from your mouth; rather you should contemplate it day and night in order that you observe to do all that is written in it; for then you will make your way successful, and then you will act wisely. Behold, I have commanded you, be strong and courageous, do not fear and lose resolve, for the Lord your God is with you wherever you will go." (Joshua 1:8-9)

Those words to Joshua resonate for Israel in our times as well, more than ever, as do the words of the prophet Isaiah, which are a call to action, not just for the entire Jewish people around the world, but for all supporters of Zion:

"For Zion's sake, I will not be silent..." (Isaiah 62:1)

The message is clear for all of us. May we all be worthy of accomplishing the tasks before us, for Israel, and for the world.

Appendix

- Glossary
- The Hebrew Calendar
- Projects of the Shiloh Israel Children's Fund
- Credits
- Acknowledgments

Glossary

Aliyah – the term (lit. going up) used to describe the immigration of Jews to the Land of Israel.

Ashkenazim – the term used to describe the Jews of northern and eastern European background.

Balfour Declaration – the 1917 declaration by British Foreign Minister Balfour supporting the establishment of a Jewish State in Palestine (the Land of Israel, including all of what is now controlled by Israel and Jordan). The Balfour Declaration was eventually endorsed by the League of Nations, after its establishment in 1920.

Bar (or Bat) Mitzvah – (lit. son [or daughter] of the commandments) the event at which one reaches the age (13 [or 12]) of Jewish religious maturity and responsibility for following God's commandments.

Children of Israel – (sometimes translated as Israelites) the name used for the People of Israel from the Exodus until the first Exile from the Land of Israel.

Crusaders – In 1095, the Pope Urban II called on Christians to capture the Holy Land from the Muslims. Mobs of enthusiastic followers moved towards and into Israel, destroying any communities that were in their way. In 1099, they took control of Jerusalem, killing most of its non-Christian inhabitants.

Diaspora – (Greek for "scattering") term used to describe the Jewish communities that were formed around the world as a result of Israel being exiled from the Land of Israel.

Disengagement – the 2005 Israel unilateral withdrawal plan, which effectively expelled 10,000 Israeli Jews from their homes and destroyed their communities.

Even HaEzer – near the current city Rosh Ha'Ayin; the location of the war which the Children of Israel lost and in which the Ark of the Covenant was taken.

Gaza – twenty-five mile strip of land along the Mediterranean Sea that was captured by Israel in the Six Day War. In 2005, all of the Israeli communities in these areas were expelled from their homes by the Israeli government.

Haggadah – the prayerbook/storybook that is read at the Passover Seder.

Hamas – the Islamic Resistance Movement, an Islamic terror organization dedicated to the destruction of the State of Israel through whatever means possible and the establishment of an Islamic state in its place. Recent evidence has revealed substantial Hamas fundraising activity in the United States and Europe and strong links with other terror organizations such as Al Qaeda and Hezbollah. In 2006, Hamas was elected as the dominant faction in the P.A. governing body.

Holocaust – the systematic slaughter of six million Jews by the Nazis in Europe during World War II.

I.D.F. – Israel Defense Forces

Jihad – term in Arabic literally meaning "Holy War." In practice, it refers almost exclusively to the armed struggle against the non- Muslims.

Knesset – the Israeli Parliament, consisting of 120 members.

Kabbalah – a discipline and school of thought discussing the mystical aspect of Judaism. It is a set of esoteric teachings meant to define the inner meaning of both the Tanach (Hebrew Bible) and traditional Rabbinic literature, as well as to explain the deep significance of Jewish religious observances.

League of Nations – the European-dominated body, which was a precursor to the United Nations.

Matzah – unleavened bread eaten on Passover.

Midrash – an analysis and exploration, often using homilies, to examine the lessons of the Bible.

P.A. – the Palestinian Authority, established as part of the Oslo Accords in 1993 to be the governing body for the Arabs of Judea, Samaria, and Gaza.

PLO – the Palestine Liberation Organization, (the forerunner of the Palestinian Authority), formed in 1964 by the Arabs of the Land of Israel under the leadership of Yasser Arafat, for the purpose of destroying the

State of Israel through whatever means necessary. In 1993, the PLO signed the Oslo Accords with the State of Israel, but its dominant Fatah faction continued to carry out a majority of the terror attacks against Israeli civilians.

Passover Seder – the festive, experiential meal on the first night (first two nights outside of Israel) of the Passover holiday, in which Jews commemorate and celebrate the Exodus from slavery in Egypt.

Religious Zionism – the movement of Jews returning to the Land of Israel and establishing the State of Israel as an important first step of the ingathering of the exiles and the process of redemption, all in accordance with Biblical Prophecy.

Rosh Ha'Ayin – a city northeast of Tel Aviv, originally populated almost entirely by Yemenite Jewish immigrants.

Rosh HaShanah – the two-day holiday commemorating the New Year on the Hebrew calendar. It is traditionally a holiday of both festivity and introspection.

Sephardim – the term used to describe the Jews of Spanish and Mediterranean background.

Shabbat – the seventh day of the week, observed by religious Jews as the day of rest. In English, called the Sabbath, it begins on Friday evening at sunset until Saturday night at nightfall. It is a special day set aside for devotion to God and His Torah within the context of family and prayer.

Shechem – the Arab-populated city in Samaria where the Biblical Joseph and his sons Ephraim and Manasseh are buried. The city is known to the Arabs and most of the world as Nablus.

Shmoneh Esreh – the thrice daily silent prayer which is the core of the Jewish prayer service. Its contents summarize the elements of Jewish prayer.

Sifri Zuta – a Midrash on the Book of Numbers.

Tabernacle – the central place of worship for the Children of Israel, first in the Sinai desert and then in the Land of Israel, before the building of the Temple in Jerusalem.

Tachanun – the short weekday afternoon prayer bemoaning the downtrodden state of the scattered nation of Israel.

Talmud – the Oral Law; a series of explanations and instructions passed down from Moses through the generations to clarify the instructions in the Written Law (the Five Books of Moses).

Tanach – the Five Books of Moses (Pentateuch), the Writings of the Prophets, and the other Writings of the Old Testament.

Torah – the Five Books of Moses, sometimes refers also to the Writings of the Prophets, the other Writings of the Old Testament, and the broad spectrum of commentaries, including the Talmud.

West Bank – relatively recent term coined by the Arabs and most of the Western world to describe the Biblical areas of Judea and Samaria, liberated by the State of Israel in the Six Day War.

Yom Kippur – the Day of Atonement, the most solemn day in the Hebrew calendar; a day of introspection, fasting, and prayer.

Zionism – the movement of Jews returning to the Land of Israel and establishing the State of Israel.

The Hebrew Calendar

The Hebrew calendar is lunisolar, with the months being counted according to the moon, and the years according to the sun. Every two or three years, there is an extra month of Adar, known as Adar II.

1. Tishrei – generally corresponds to September-October
Holidays – Rosh HaShanah, Yom Kippur, Sukkot (Feast of Tabernacles)

2. Heshvan – generally corresponds to October-November
Holidays – None

3. Kislev – generally corresponds to November-December
Holidays – Hannukah

4. Tevet – generally corresponds to December-January
Holidays – None

5. Shvat – generally corresponds to January-February
Holidays – Tu B'Shvat (Holiday of Trees)

6. Adar – generally corresponds to February-March
Holidays – Purim

7. Nissan – generally corresponds to March-April
Holidays – Passover

8. Iyar – generally corresponds to April-May
Holidays and Days of Introspection/Mourning – Memorial Day, Israel Independence Day, Jerusalem Day, Lag B'Omer

9. Sivan – generally corresponds to May-June
Holidays – Shavuot

10. Tamuz – generally corresponds to June-July
Holidays – None

11. Av – generally corresponds to July-August
Holidays and Days of Introspection/Mourning – Tisha B'Av
(commemorates the destruction of the two Holy Temples in
Jerusalem, as well as other national tragedies), Tu B'Av (see
Chapter 3)

12. Elul – generally corresponds to August-September
Holidays – None; Elul is a month of introspection, with a
special focus on self-improvement leading up to Rosh
HaShanah and Yom Kippur in the month of Tishrei

Projects Of
The Shiloh Israel Children's Fund (SICF)

Therapeutic Projects

Originally established as a small child development center serving a rapidly increasing child population, the recently-expanded Therapy Center in Shiloh is becoming a beacon of light for the communities of this entire region. The center provides physical, occupational, and speech therapy on an ongoing basis for all of the children in the region, with a special focus on the needs of terror victims. In fact, the acclaimed Emotional Therapy Program, heavily supported by the Shiloh Israel Children's Fund, was started as a response to the waves of terror that have traumatized a generation of children in the heartland of Israel. Post-trauma stress has led to many children suffering from sleep problems, excessive fear of being left alone, extreme fear of traveling anywhere outside the local communities (even in bulletproof transportation), or obsession with a general fear of dying. The difficult security situation, both actual and psychological, has greatly increased the need for this magnificent program, which also treats emotional difficulties stemming from family problems, leaning disabilities, and other psychological challenges. The program uses music, artistic expression, movement, and interaction with animals for its various forms of treatment.

Animal-Assisted Therapy (AAT) is performed in the Therapeutic Petting Zoo, which hopefully will soon be expanded to include an enclosed treatment room. Therapy with Horses takes place at the Horse Farm on a hilltop adjacent to the Center. SICF has created a harmonious and integrative arrangement between the Center and all of these other components of the overall Therapeutic Program. The result is a network of wonderful working relationships that serve the needs of the children.

Educational Projects

As discussed earlier, the educational system as a whole isn't being given the priority it deserves. In many parts of Israel and specifically in the secular school system, the People of the Book have become a caricature, as the children of the "kingdom of ministers" are sent home from school at 12 noon with absolutely no religious learning.

For the children of the heartland, where religious learning and prayer is valued, and most parents pay extra to give their children an extended school day, the problem is quite different. As a result of the international pressures on Israel, as well as the unfortunate internal controversy regarding our right to dwell in the Biblical heartland, Shiloh and the entire region of Samaria have suffered from insufficient educational funding for a young and rapidly growing student population. Therefore, many basic educational needs are not being taken care of by the authorities. In addition, the stress caused by the constant fear of terror attacks has created a new and difficult educational reality, requiring hands-on and therapeutic programs to meet these needs. The children of Gush Shiloh, the Shiloh bloc of communities, deserve no less than children anywhere, an education to nurture and develop their young minds and hearts. Working together with the various leaders of the schools and nurseries in Shiloh and its vicinity, the Shiloh Israel Children's Fund is trying to create a strong educational climate by funding programs for the schools that will, God-willing, mold the future political and spiritual leaders of Israel, as well as leaders in all other fields. Most importantly, these children will grow up to be solid citizens of Israel, dedicated both to God's Torah, and to His Land.

Recreational Projects

People in the United States and much of the Western world often take playgrounds and parks for granted. True, they recognize the importance of recreation, but in the Israeli communities that have been suffering from terrorist shootings on the roads, rocket attacks, and bombings, nothing can be taken for granted anymore. In the

Samaria region, where Shiloh is located, families hesitate before loading their children into the family car for a drive to one of the big parks in the city. The shootings on the roads have not only torn families apart by creating many orphans and widows, but have also robbed the children of these communities of the innocence of childhood. Therefore, it is essential that there be sufficient recreational opportunities within these communities. The Shiloh Israel Children's Fund is trying to push forward a parks and playgrounds project to create a variety of recreational areas for children of all ages in Gush Shiloh. Another important, ongoing project is our summer camp program, in which we lengthen the standard Israeli day camp from three to at least five weeks and provide adult staff and supervision. This is a vital respite from the challenge of "what to do with the children" in the hot, unstructured summer months.

All of these projects are developed with the needs of the children first and foremost, and are evaluated and reevaluated on an ongoing basis to ensure their success.

The support of all caring people is welcome!

Contact Information:

S.I.C.F Website: www.shilohisraelchildren.org

Email: david@shilohisraelchildren.org

Donations:
Shiloh Israel Children's Fund
P.O. Box 212
Suffern, N.Y. 10901

Credits

All photographs in the book, including the front cover photograph, are by David Rubin, except as noted below:

Page 8:	Map courtesy of the Israel Antiquities Authority Archives: British Mandate Record Files: file no.171, Seilun, Kh.
Page 11:	Photograph by Joe Bazer
Page 42:	Map courtesy of Menachem Brody photo@shechem.org
Page 46:	Map reprinted with permission from Biblical Studies Press www.bible.org
Page 48:	Tu B'Av illustration by Gretta Kuznetsov
Page 90:	Map prepared by Frumi Hasidim
Page 94:	Courtesy of Chanah Hoffbauer from her collection of photos - photographer unknown
Page 101:	Photograph courtesy of the Israel Antiquities Authority
Page 104:	Photograph by Batya Medad
Page 106:	Photograph on bottom: Courtesy of the Shiloh excavation team, Bar Ilan University
Page 118:	Photograph courtesy of Menachem Brody photo@shechem.org
Page 120:	Photograph courtesy of Reuters
Page 127:	Photographer unknown
Page 128:	Photograph courtesy of Flash 90
Page 129:	Photograph on top courtesy of Zoom 77
Page 129:	Photographer unknown for bottom photograph
Back Cover:	Photograph by Avital Rubin

Acknowledgments

There are many people who volunteered their time or knowledge in various ways and I have great *Hakarat Hatov* (appreciation) for their contributions. You all know who you are and I thank you for your participation in this project.

Before specifically acknowledging anyone, I want to thank the King of the Universe: Thank you for bringing me back to Your Land, to Your people, and to Your Torah, which always provides me with the guidance to navigate the challenges of life.

There are several people whose efforts are worthy of special mention:

To Rabbi Elchanan Bin-Nun and Rabbi Zuriel Wiener, thank you for your Biblical and Halachic insights.

For sharing your extensive knowledge about the spiritual/historical significance of Shiloh, a special thank you to Rabbi Dov Berkovits, who assisted with both proofreading and Biblical concepts.

For proofreading and for offering valuable suggestions, many thanks to Chanah Ben Yochanan.

To Rosemary Schindler, thank you for the original inspiration and encouragement.

Many thanks to Mr. Yussie Stern, whose selfless dedication to SICF freed up some of my time to work on this project.

To my children, thank you for the unconditional love and the occasional quiet outside my office.

To my mother, Frieda Rubin, who together with my father, Ruby Rubin, of blessed memory, always somehow raised me to pursue my dreams.

Last but not least, thank you to my wife Lisa, for sharing my passion for this project, for putting up with my many hours on the computer, and for the many valuable suggestions. Most importantly, thank you for being my partner in the challenges, pains, and pleasures of life.

I would also like to note that in supplementing my own knowledge of Biblical Hebrew to formulate the English translations of the Biblical sources used in this book, I referred to *The Stone Edition Tanach of the Art Scroll Series* (Mesorah), *The Jerusalem Bible* (Koren), and *Judaica Books of the Prophets* (Judaica Press).

Other Books By David Rubin

Available online at www.DavidRubinIsrael.com/books/
~ Phone orders 1-800-431-1579 ~ Or at a bookstore near you!

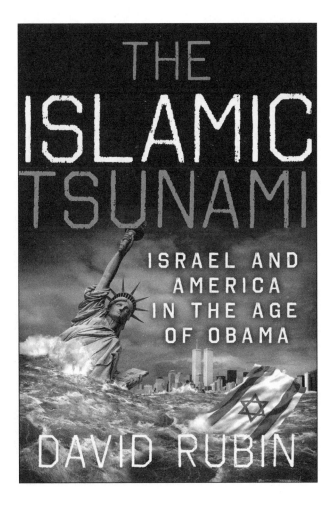

The Islamic Tsunami
Israel And America In The Age Of Obama
ISBN: 978-0-9829067-0-5

Available online at www.DavidRubinIsrael.com/books/
~ Phone orders 1-800-431-1579 ~ Or at a bookstore near you!

Peace For Peace
Israel In The New Middle East
ISBN: 978-0-9829067-4-3

Available online at www.DavidRubinIsrael.com/books/
~ Phone orders 1-800-431-1579 ~ Or at a bookstore near you!

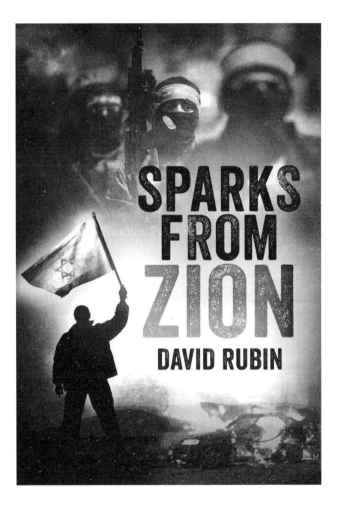

Sparks From Zion

ISBN: 978-0-9829067-6-7